UNITED NATIONS OFFICE ON DRUGS AND CRIME
Vienna

Handbook on
Criminal Justice Responses to Terrorism

CRIMINAL JUSTICE HANDBOOK SERIES

UNITED NATIONS
New York, 2009

Acknowledgements

The *Handbook on Criminal Justice Responses to Terrorism* was finalized drawing on texts prepared by Yvon Dandurand (Dean of Research and Industry Liaison, University of the Fraser Valley, Canada; and Senior Associate, International Centre for Criminal Law Reform and Criminal Justice Policy) under a consultancy contract for the United Nations Office on Drugs and Crime (UNODC).

The draft text was reviewed at an expert group meeting held at UNODC headquarters in Vienna on 1 and 2 October 2007. UNODC wishes to acknowledge the valuable contributions received from the following experts who participated in that meeting: Christian Ahlund, Andrea Bianchi, Marvin Carvajal Perez, Anne Charbord, Michael De Feo, Helen Duffy, Anton du Plessis, Mark Ellis, John Grieve, Tiyanjana Maluwa, Joanne Mariner, Veronica Milinchuk, Vivienne O'Connor, Robin Palmer, Andrew Powell, Cathy Powell, Colette Rausch, Rachid Sadouk, Mark Shaw, Masamba Sita and Jayampathy Wickramaratne.

This publication was financed drawing on funds provided by the following countries, having made voluntary contributions to the UNODC Global Project on Strengthening the Legal Regime against Terrorism: Austria, Belgium, Canada, Colombia, Denmark, France, Germany, Greece, Italy, Japan, Liechtenstein, Monaco, Netherlands, New Zealand, Norway, Spain, Sweden, Switzerland, Turkey, United Kingdom of Great Britain and Northern Ireland and United States of America.

UNITED NATIONS PUBLICATION
Sales No. E.09.IV.2
ISBN 978-92-1-130270-7

Contents

Part Three
Criminal justice accountability and oversight mechanisms

Part one

Introduction and legal context

I. Introduction

An effective and prevention-focused response to terrorism should include a strong criminal justice element: one that is guided by a normative legal framework and embedded in the core principles of the rule of law, due process and respect for human rights. Perpetrators of terrorist acts as defined in the universal legal instruments against terrorism are criminals, and they should therefore be dealt with by the criminal justice process as it is the most appropriate and fair mechanism to ensure that justice is achieved and that the rights of the accused are protected. In addition to this core function, criminal justice approaches to terrorism also provide for effective prevention mechanisms, including interventions that target the funding of terrorists and terrorist organizations and allow for the interception of conspiracies to commit attacks and the prohibition of incitement to terrorism.

To provide an effective criminal justice response to terrorism, States need adequately functioning counter-terrorism legal regimes and criminal justice systems, as well as the related capacity to deal with potentially complex criminal cases and engage effectively in international criminal justice cooperation. This requires a firm commitment by States to pursue common objectives at the national, subregional and regional levels.

An essential part of a comprehensive criminal justice response is the widespread ratification and implementation of the universal legal instruments against terrorism (meaning simply the relevant multilateral treaties and supplemental agreements). In this regard, the technical assistance provided by the United Nations Office on Drugs and Crime (UNODC) is particularly important as it supports not only the efforts of Member States to ratify and implement the relevant counter-terrorism instruments, but also their efforts to strengthen the rule of law and build the capacity of their law enforcement and criminal justice officials to apply these laws effectively and appropriately.

UNODC is cognizant of the need for a holistic approach to address the complex issue of terrorism, i.e. one which, in addition to criminal justice responses, also includes instruments and frameworks that address the socio-economic and political conditions conducive to the spread of terrorism from a prevention perspective. These, however, are not being addressed in the present *Handbook on Criminal Justice Responses to Terrorism*, which focuses on criminal justice responses only.

The *Handbook* aims to provide law enforcement and criminal justice officials with an accessible guide to assist them in dealing with some of the key issues that they face in their efforts to respond to terrorist and related crimes. The *Handbook* will also be of use to policymakers and political leaders in the shaping of new or enhanced counter-terrorism laws, policies and practices. It reviews the many challenges encountered by the various components of the criminal justice system in the prevention, investigation, prosecution and detention of alleged or convicted perpetrators of terrorist crimes. It offers guidance based on international standards and generally accepted good practices.

As a practical tool, the *Handbook* can be used to facilitate the implementation of the universal legal instruments against terrorism within the context of accepted criminal justice and rule-of-law principles and practices, particularly as these apply in the fight against terrorism. It can be used to support a review of the capacity of a criminal justice system in a particular country, guide policy development or support training initiatives.

The *Handbook* forms part of a set of technical assistance tools that have been developed by UNODC. Other tools specifically related to the ratification and implementation of the universal legal instruments against terrorism are also available from UNODC. They include the updated Legislative Guide to the Universal Legal Regime against Terrorism;[1] the Guide for the Legislative Incorporation and Implementation of the Universal Anti-Terrorism Instruments; Preventing Terrorist Acts: a Criminal Justice Strategy Integrating Rule of Law Standards in Implementation of United Nations Anti-Terrorism Instruments; and the electronic legal resources on international terrorism.

In addition, a number of other tools are available from UNODC to assist in strengthening the rule of law and national criminal justice systems, including the *Compendium of United Nations Standards and Norms in Crime Prevention and Criminal Justice*, as well as the *Criminal Justice Assessment Toolkit*, which proposes a standardized and cross-referenced set of tools designed to assist practitioners in conducting comprehensive assessments of criminal justice systems. These and other tools are listed in the annex to the *Handbook*, together with information on how they can be obtained.

The *Handbook* is divided into three parts. Part one presents, in general terms, the role of criminal justice systems in the fight against terrorism, as well as the international legal framework that should govern this role. Part two considers each main component of the criminal justice system and the issues and challenges relating to counter-terrorism. It contains chapters dealing with the challenges faced by policymakers, law enforcement agencies, prosecutors, defence counsel, the judiciary and correctional authorities, and ends with a general discussion (which is applicable to all components of the criminal justice system) of the imperative to protect victims' rights. Part three describes accountability and oversight mechanisms for all of these components.

---

[1] United Nations publication, Sales No. E.04.V.7.

II. Importance of an effective rule of law-based criminal justice response to terrorism

Terrorism is a complex and ever-changing phenomenon. Its motivations, financing and support mechanisms, methods of attack and choice of targets are constantly evolving, thus adding to the complexity of an effective strategy to counter it. Moreover, its increasingly transnational nature requires enhanced criminal justice cooperation among States to deny safe havens to those who commit or attempt to commit terrorist crimes. Terrorism has truly become a global threat that requires a global and prevention-focused response. This should include a broad range of short- and long-term initiatives, ranging from addressing underlying conditions conducive to the spread of terrorism to building state capacity to prevent and combat it.

To the extent that counter-terrorist activities are grounded in an efficient criminal justice process that respects the principles of rule of law and human rights, they can offer a peaceful, accountable and legitimate response to terrorism. This kind of criminal justice response to terrorism can help avoid an escalation of violence and the use of force outside the protections and procedural guarantees offered by the due process of law. It can reinforce a society's commitment to the rule of law and human rights, even when under terrorist threats.

The role of the criminal justice system in countering terrorism is a challenging one. Indeed, the primary objective of counter-terrorism strategies must be to prevent terrorist incidents from taking place. The reality, however, is that many criminal justice systems are currently better at responding to and punishing crimes after the fact than at preventing them in the first place. Often, existing criminal justice practices are ineffective when it comes to preventing terrorist conspiracies from achieving their aim. A forward-looking, preventive criminal justice strategy against terrorist violence requires a comprehensive system of substantive offences, investigative powers and techniques, evidentiary rules and international cooperation. The goal is to proactively integrate substantive and procedural mechanisms to reduce the incidence and severity of terrorist violence, and to do so within the strict constraints and protections of the criminal justice system and the rule of law.

Criminal justice systems have approached these challenges differently, depending on their legal tradition, their level of development, their relative institutional sophistication and their own circumstances. In some instances, a perceived urgent need to respond to a specific threat has led States to improvise new approaches and, in so doing, stretch the limits of their criminal law and due processes to the extreme. Furthermore, many criminal justice systems have to devote considerable efforts to increasing the effectiveness of their terrorism prevention measures and, in particular, their ability to cooperate at the international level with various counter-terrorism initiatives. This has resulted in additional stress being placed on the already limited capacity of many criminal justice systems and has perhaps weakened or compromised their ability to function within basic rule of law and human rights principles.

The United Nations has responded to requests by Member States for assistance to enhance their criminal justice capacity to respond to terrorism. UNODC is one of the United Nations main providers of technical assistance in this regard. In addition to the specialized services to strengthen the international legal regime against terrorism, provided by its Terrorism Prevention Branch, UNODC can draw on its specialized technical competence in crime prevention, criminal justice and rule-of-law issues; its wealth of experience in promoting and facilitating international cooperation in criminal matters; its expertise and experience in assisting countries to build up and enhance the capacity of national criminal justice systems; its operational capacity and field presence; and the programmatic synergy of its efforts for dealing with drug control, transnational organized crime, money-laundering and corruption.

Rule of law and human rights

In his speech to the Security Council's Counter-Terrorism Committee on 6 March 2003, the then Secretary-General, Mr. Kofi Annan, emphasized the need "to develop an inter-national programme of action, founded on an unshakeable commitment to upholding the rule of law" and further stated that "as terrorism involves the calculated use of violence in violation of the law, our response to terrorism should aim to ensure the rule of law".

The report of the Secretary-General to the Security Council on the rule of law and transitional justice in conflict and post-conflict societies reiterates that the "rule of law" is a concept that lies at the very heart of the mission of the United Nations: "It refers to a principle of governance in which all persons, institutions and entities, public and private, including the State itself, are accountable to laws that are publicly promulgated, equally enforced and independently adjudicated, and which are consistent with international human rights norms and standards."[2]

Terrorism threatens both the rule of law and the fundamental freedoms of citizens and entire societies. At the same time, inappropriate counter-terrorism responses may also undermine important rule of law and human rights principles. Resolutions adopted by consensus over the past few years by the General Assembly[3] and the Commission on Human Rights[4] have reaffirmed the threshold requirement that counter-terrorism measures must comply with international law, including international human rights, refugee and humanitarian law. They have also conveyed a strong message that respecting human rights while countering terrorism is not only a matter of legal obligation but also essential to the ultimate success of any counter-terrorism strategy.[5] In its resolution 1456 (2003), the Security Council reaffirmed the same general principle: "States must ensure that any measures taken to combat terrorism comply with all their obligations under international law, and should adopt such measures in accordance with international law, in particular international human rights, refugee and humanitarian law."[6] The Security Council reiterated that obligation in paragraph 4 of its resolution 1624 (2005).

---

[2]S/2004/616, para. 6.

[3]General Assembly resolution 59/191. See also General Assembly resolution 60/158.

[4]Commission on Human Rights resolution 2004/87.

[5]Edward J. Flynn, "Counter-terrorism and human rights: the view from the United Nations", *European Human Rights Law Review*, No. 1, 2005, p. 30.

[6]See also Security Council resolution 1566 (2004).

"Terrorism flourishes in environments of despair, humiliation, poverty, political oppression, extremism and human rights abuse; it also flourishes in contexts of regional conflict and foreign occupation; and it profits from weak State capacity to maintain law and order."

Report of the High-level Panel on Threats, Challenges and Change
(A/59/565 and Corr.1, para. 145).

Other international and regional organizations have also formally affirmed the crucial importance of respecting the rule of law and human rights in preventing terrorism. For example, article 15 of the Inter-American Convention against Terrorism,[7] states that the measures carried out by the States parties under the Convention shall take place with full respect for the rule of law, human rights and fundamental freedoms. Article 22 of the Organization of African Unity Convention on the Prevention and Combating of Terrorism[8] of 1999 stipulates that counter-terrorism measures described in the Convention must be implemented in a manner consistent with the general principles of international law, in particular the principles of international humanitarian law, as well as the African Charter on Human and Peoples' Rights.[9] Finally, the Council of Europe Guidelines on Human Rights and the Fight against Terrorism[10] emphasize the need to prevent and prohibit arbitrariness and ensure the lawfulness of all anti-terrorist measures. The Guidelines reaffirm that all measures taken by States to fight terrorism must respect human rights and the principle of the rule of law, while excluding any form of arbitrariness, as well as any discriminatory or racist treatment, and must be subject to appropriate supervision.

The 2006 United Nations Global Counter-Terrorism Strategy[11] also underlines the inextricable links between human rights and security and reaffirms the important role of the United Nations system in strengthening the international legal architecture by promoting the rule of law, respect for human rights and effective criminal justice systems, which constitute the fundamental basis of the common fight against terrorism. The Strategy incorporates a number of important measures to ensure respect for human rights for all and for the rule of law as the fundamental basis of the fight against terrorism. The Strategy's plan of action includes a commitment to:

> make every effort to develop and maintain an effective and rule of law-based national criminal justice system that can ensure, in accordance with our obligations under international law, that any person who participates in the financing, planning, preparation or perpetration of terrorist acts or in support of terrorist acts is brought to justice, on the basis of the principle to extradite or prosecute, with due respect for human rights and fundamental freedoms, and that such terrorist acts are established as serious criminal offences in domestic laws and regulations.[12]

In the Strategy's plan of action, the General Assembly recognizes that States might require assistance in developing and maintaining effective and rule of law-based criminal justice systems and encourages them to resort to the technical assistance delivered, inter alia, by UNODC. The assistance provided must comply with the United Nations guidance note of April 2008 on a United Nations approach to rule-of-law assistance, which applies

---

[7]A/56/1002-S/2002/745, annex.

[8]United Nations, *Treaty Series*, vol. 2219, No. 39464.

[9]Ibid., vol. 1520, No. 26363.

[10]Council of Europe Guidelines on Human Rights and the Fight against Terrorism, adopted by the Committee of Ministers on 11 July 2002 at the 804th meeting of the Ministers' Deputies.

[11]General Assembly resolution 60/288.

[12]General Assembly resolution 60/288, annex, section IV, para. 4.

to United Nations rule-of-law activities and programmes in all circumstances, including crisis, post-crisis, conflict prevention, post-conflict and development contexts. In summary, United Nations rule-of-law assistance must fulfil the following obligations:

- Be based on international norms and standards;
- Take into account the political context in a particular country;
- Be based on the unique country context;
- Promote human rights and gender justice;
- Ensure national ownership;
- Support national reform constituencies;
- Ensure a coherent and comprehensive strategic approach;
- Engage in effective coordination and partnerships.

III.   Terrorism and international law

Despite being regarded by the Security Council as a threat to international peace and security, for the most part acts of international terrorism do not fall into the category of "core international" crimes such as genocide, war crimes and crimes against humanity. There are therefore no international criminal courts or tribunals with jurisdiction over these crimes.[13] Terrorist crimes (as defined in the universal instruments against terrorism) fall in the category of national criminal law of international concern. The duty to bring perpetrators of terrorism to justice therefore rests solely with national criminal justice systems. Without adequate domestic capacity to discharge that duty, international counter-terrorism efforts will almost certainly fail.

The criminal justice response to terrorism is therefore essentially framed by national law, which itself must comply with various aspects of international law. There are several components of international law that are directly relevant to the criminal justice response to terrorism. In addition to treaty-based obligations stemming from their ratification of the universal legal instruments against terrorism and several legally binding obligations imposed through the relevant Security Council resolutions on counter-terrorism, States also have a number of legal obligations under other branches of international law, including international human rights, humanitarian, refugee and customary law. These legal regimes are complementary bodies of law that share a common goal, namely, the protection of the lives, health and dignity of persons. While international humanitarian law applies only in times of armed conflict, human rights law applies at all times: in times of peace and in times of armed conflict. The concurrent application of these two bodies of law has been expressly recognized by various international tribunals and national courts.[14] More detailed information on the various relevant aspects of international law, including international criminal law, international humanitarian law, international refugee law and international human rights law will also be made available in the UNODC publication, currently in preparation, on frequently asked questions on international law aspects of countering terrorism.

It is the responsibility of all practitioners to ensure that criminal justice practices are in compliance with national law and applicable international law. Monitoring that compliance—and taking action to address non-compliance—typically falls within the ambit of legal judicial institutions (including the defence bar and prosecution services) and various institutional oversight mechanisms. Civil society and public media must also remain vigilant and assume their own responsibility in this regard.

---

[13]The International Criminal Court, created in 1998 by the Treaty of Rome, is granted jurisdiction over the crime of genocide, crimes against humanity, war crimes and the crime of aggression. Jurisdiction over acts of terrorism was rejected during the negotiations that resulted in the Court's creation.

[14]Emanuela-Chiara Gillard, ICRC Legal Adviser, International Committee of the Red Cross, statement at the International Association of Refugee Law Judges World Conference, held in Stockholm on 21-23 April 2005.

A. Universal legal regime against terrorism

It is well known that the international community has not yet been able to agree on a comprehensive definition of terrorism despite several attempts by the General Assembly and the Security Council in this regard. Most notably, in 1994 the General Assembly, in the Declaration on Measures to Eliminate International Terrorism, declared that criminal acts intended or calculated to provoke a state of terror in the general public, a group of persons or particular persons for political purposes are in any circumstances unjustifiable, whatever the consideration of a political, philosophical, ideological, racial, ethnic, religious or other nature that may be invoked to justify them.[15] In 2004, the Security Council, in its resolution 1566 (2004), identified elements of a definition, referring to "criminal acts, including against civilians, committed with the intent to cause death or serious bodily injury, or taking of hostages, with the purpose to provoke a state of terror in the general public or in a group of persons or particular persons, intimidate a population or compel a government or an international organization to do or abstain from doing any act".[16]

Currently, Member States are negotiating a draft comprehensive convention on international terrorism. The convention would complement the existing framework of universal instruments against terrorism and would build on key guiding principles already present in that regime. Those principles include the following: the importance of the criminalization of terrorist offences, making them punishable by law and calling for the prosecution or extradition of the perpetrators; the need to eliminate legislation that establishes exceptions to such criminalization on political, philosophical, ideological, racial, ethnic, religious or similar grounds; a strong call for Member States to take action to prevent terrorist acts; and an emphasis on the need for Member States to cooperate, exchange information and provide each other with the greatest measure of assistance in the prevention, investigation and prosecution of terrorist acts.

However, the lack of a broad definition of terrorism does not present a legal challenge to practitioners. Since 1963, the international community has elaborated a comprehensive set of universal legal instruments to prevent terrorist acts. They consist of more than a dozen conventions and protocols covering almost every conceivable kind of terrorist act. Those legal instruments (16 in total as of 2008), together with several Security Council resolutions relating to terrorism (most notably, resolutions 1267 (1999), 1373 (2001) and 1540 (2004), see below), make up what is commonly referred to as the universal legal regime against terrorism.

The universal legal instruments were developed under the auspices of the United Nations and its specialized agencies, in particular the International Civil Aviation Organization, the International Maritime Organization and the International Atomic Energy Agency, and are open to participation by all Member States. They are based on a condemnation of international terrorism as endangering international security and world peace. The most recent instruments were adopted in 2005 in the form of substantive changes to three of first 13 instruments, including the Amendment to the Convention on the Physical Protection of Nuclear Material[17] and amendments to both the Protocol of 2005 to the Convention for the Suppression of Unlawful Acts against the Safety of Maritime

---

[15]General Assembly resolution 49/60, annex.

[16]Security Council resolution 1566 (2004), para. 3.

[17]Adopted on 8 July 2005 by the Conference to Consider and Adopt Proposed Amendments to the Convention on the Physical Protection of Nuclear Material.

Navigation[18] and the Protocol of 2005 to the Protocol for the Suppression of Unlawful Acts against the Safety of Fixed Platforms Located on the Continental Shelf.[19]

The 16 instruments cover the following unlawful terrorist acts:

- Acts of aircraft hijacking;
- Acts of aviation sabotage;
- Acts of violence at airports;
- Acts against the safety of maritime navigation;
- Acts against the safety of fixed platforms located on the continental shelf;
- Crime against internationally protected persons (such as the kidnapping of diplomats);
- Acts of unlawful taking and possession of nuclear material;
- Acts of hostage-taking;
- Acts of terrorist bombings;
- Acts of funding of the commission of terrorist acts and terrorist organizations;
- Nuclear terrorism by individuals and groups.

These instruments create, inter alia, obligations for States parties to adopt substantive criminal and procedural criminal law measures to counter various acts of terrorism, as well as administrative measures to combat the financing of terrorism. The goal of these instruments is to ensure that criminal justice practitioners are equipped with effective mechanisms to lawfully prevent and punish acts of terrorism. These measures are designed to have both a preventive and a dissuasive impact on terrorism.

The dissuasive aspect of these international instruments is based in part on an attempt to harmonize the criminal legislation of States and to strengthen law enforcement and criminal justice cooperation. Effective criminalization of terrorist behaviour by all States is meant to eliminate safe havens for perpetrators of terrorist crimes and to facilitate international cooperation among State agencies involved in the fight against terrorism.

In some instances, the universal instruments expressly require compliance with various aspects of human rights law. The International Convention for the Suppression of the Financing of Terrorism,[20] for example, includes several such requirements as well as an article (art. 21) that makes it clear that the Convention does not affect other rights, obligations and responsibilities of States under international law.

The universal instruments do not define terrorist offences as crimes under international law. They simply create an obligation for States parties to criminalize the offences in question under their domestic law, exercise jurisdiction over offenders under prescribed conditions and provide for international cooperation mechanisms that enable States parties to either prosecute or extradite the alleged offender.

---

[18]Adopted on 14 October 2005 by the Diplomatic Conference on the Revision of the SUA Treaties (LEG/CONF.15/21).

[19]Adopted on 14 October 2005 by the Diplomatic Conference on the Revision of the SUA Treaties (LEG/CONF.15/22).

[20]United Nations, *Treaty Series*, vol. 2178, No. 38349.

Universal instruments against terrorism at a glance

1963   Convention on Offences and Certain Other Acts Committed On Board Aircraft

- Applies to acts affecting in-flight safety.

- Authorizes the aircraft commander to impose reasonable measures, including restraint, on any person he or she has reason to believe has committed or is about to commit such an act, where necessary to protect the safety of the aircraft.

- Requires contracting States to take custody of offenders and to return control of the aircraft to the lawful commander.

1970   Convention for the Suppression of Unlawful Seizure of Aircraft

- Makes it an offence for any person on board an aircraft in flight to "unlawfully, by force or threat thereof, or any other form of intimidation, [to] seize or exercise control of that aircraft" or to attempt to do so.

- Requires parties to the Convention to make hijackings punishable by "severe penalties".

- Requires parties that have custody of offenders to either extradite the offender or submit the case for prosecution.

- Requires parties to assist each other in connection with criminal proceedings brought under the Convention.

1971   Convention for the Suppression of Unlawful Acts against the Safety of Civil Aviation

- Makes it an offence for any person unlawfully and intentionally to perform an act of violence against a person on board an aircraft in flight, if that act is likely to endanger the safety of the aircraft; to place an explosive device on an aircraft; to attempt such acts; or to be an accomplice of a person who performs or attempts to perform such acts.

- Requires parties to the Convention to make offences punishable by "severe penalties".

- Requires parties that have custody of offenders to either extradite the offender or submit the case for prosecution.

1973   Convention on the Prevention and Punishment of Crimes against Internationally Protected Persons, including Diplomatic Agents

- Defines an "internationally protected person" as a Head of State, Minister for Foreign Affairs, representative or official of a State or international organization who is entitled to special protection in a foreign State, and his or her family.

- Requires parties to criminalize and make punishable "by appropriate penalties which take into account their grave nature" the intentional murder, kidnapping or other attack upon the person or liberty of an internationally protected person, a violent attack upon the official premises, the private accommodations or the means of transport of such person; a threat or attempt to commit such an attack; and an act "constituting participation as an accomplice"

1979   International Convention against the Taking of Hostages

- Provides that "any person who seizes or detains and threatens to kill, to injure or to continue to detain another person in order to compel a third party, namely, a State, an international intergovernmental organization, a natural or juridical person, or a group of persons, to do or abstain from doing any act as an explicit or implicit condition for the release of the hostage commits the offence of taking of hostages within the meaning of this Convention".

1980   Convention on the Physical Protection of Nuclear Material

- Criminalizes the unlawful possession, use, transfer or theft of nuclear material and threats to use nuclear material to cause death, serious injury or substantial property damage.

- Amendments to the Convention on the Physical Protection of Nuclear Material add the following:

   Make it legally binding for States parties to protect nuclear facilities and material in peaceful domestic use, storage and transport;

   Provides for expanded cooperation between and among States regarding rapid measures to locate and recover stolen or smuggled nuclear material, mitigate any radiological consequences or sabotage and prevent and combat related offences.

1988   Protocol for the Suppression of Unlawful Acts of Violence at Airports Serving International Civil Aviation, supplementary to the Convention for the Suppression of Unlawful Acts against the Safety of Civil Aviation

- Extends the provisions of the Convention for the Suppression of Unlawful Acts against the Safety of Civil Aviation to encompass terrorist acts at airports serving international civil aviation.

1988   Convention for the Suppression of Unlawful Acts against the Safety of Maritime Navigation

- Establishes a legal regime applicable to acts against the safety of international maritime navigation that is similar to the regimes established for international aviation.

- Makes it an offence for a person unlawfully and intentionally to seize or exercise control over a ship by force, threat or intimidation; to perform an act of violence against a person on board a ship if that act is likely to endanger the safe navigation of the ship; to place a destructive device or substance aboard a ship; or commit other acts against the safety of ships.

- The Protocol of 2005 to the Convention for the Suppression of Unlawful Acts against the Safety of Maritime Navigation criminalizes the use of a ship to further an act of terrorism; the transport of various materials with the knowledge or intent that they will be used to cause death or serious injury or damage; the transport on board a ship of persons who have committed an act of terrorism.

1988   Protocol for the Suppression of Unlawful Acts against the Safety of Fixed Platforms Located on the Continental Shelf

- Establishes a legal regime applicable to acts against fixed platforms on the continental shelf that is similar to the regimes established against international aviation.

- The Protocol of 2005 to the Protocol for the Suppression of Unlawful Acts against the Safety of Fixed Platforms Located on the Continental Shelf adapted the changes to the Convention for the Suppression of Unlawful Acts against the Safety of Maritime Navigation to the context of fixed platforms located on the continental shelf.

1991   Convention on the Marking of Plastic Explosives for the Purpose of Detection

- Designed to control and limit the use of unmarked and undetectable plastic explosives (negotiated subsequent to the 1988 bombing of Pan Am flight 103).

- Parties are obligated to ensure effective control, in their respective territories, over "unmarked plastic explosives".

International Convention for the Suppression of Terrorist Bombings

- Creates a regime of expanded jurisdiction over the unlawful and intentional use of explosives and other lethal devices in, into or against various defined public places with intent to kill or cause serious bodily injury, or with intent to cause extensive destruction of the public place.

1999   International Convention for the Suppression of the Financing of Terrorism

- Requires parties to take steps to prevent and counteract the direct and indirect financing of terrorists.

- Commits States to hold those who finance terrorism criminally, civilly or administratively liable for such acts.

- Provides for the identification, freezing and seizure of funds allocated for terrorist activities, as well as for the sharing of the forfeited funds with other States on a case-by-case basis. Bank secrecy is no longer adequate justification for refusing to cooperate.

2005   International Convention for the Suppression of Acts of Nuclear Terrorism

- Covers a broad range of acts and possible targets including nuclear power plants and nuclear reactors.

- Covers threats and attempts to commit such crimes or to participate in them as an accomplice.

- Stipulates that offenders shall be either extradited or prosecuted.

- Encourages States to cooperate in preventing terrorist attacks by sharing information and assisting each other in connection with criminal investigations and extradition proceedings.

- Deals with both crisis situations (assisting States to solve the situation) and post-crisis situations (rendering nuclear material safe through the International Atomic Energy Agency).

Another core part of the global legal regime to counter terrorism is a series of Security Council resolutions relating to terrorism, many of which were adopted under the authority of Chapter VII of the Charter of the United Nations, which empowers the Security Council to adopt resolutions that are legally binding on all United Nations Member States.

Most prominent among those resolutions is resolution 1373 (2001), adopted immediately following the terrorist attacks on the United States of America on 11 September 2001, which imposes extensive counter-terrorism legal obligations on all States. Its binding provisions require every country to freeze the financial assets of those who commit or attempt to commit acts of terrorism and their supporters, deny them travel or safe haven and prevent terrorist recruitment and weapons supply. In its resolution, the Council also established that all States shall "ensure that any person who participates in the financing, planning, preparation or perpetration of terrorist acts or in supporting terrorist acts is brought to justice and ensure that, in addition to any other measures against them, such terrorist acts are established as serious criminal offences in domestic laws and regulations and that the punishment duly reflects the seriousness of such terrorist acts".[21]

Furthermore, resolution 1373 (2001) obliges countries to afford one another "the greatest measure of assistance" in investigating and prosecuting terrorist acts and calls upon Member States to sign and ratify the international conventions and protocols against terrorism. In resolution 1373 (2001), the Council also created the Counter-Terrorism Committee. Later, the Security Council, through resolution 1535 (2004), established the Counter-Terrorism Committee Executive Directorate to support the work of the Committee.

Security Council resolution 1373 (2001) was preceded and followed up by several other Council resolutions relating to terrorism, including resolutions 1267 (1999), 1456 (2003),

---

[21]Security Council resolution 1373 (2001), para. 2 *(e)*.

1535 (2004), 1540 (2004) and 1566 (2004). Resolution 1267 (1999) deals with the imposition of sanctions against the Taliban and Al-Qaida (including freezing of assets, an arms embargo and a travel ban). It has subsequently been followed up and expanded by resolutions 1333 (2000), 1390 (2002), 1455 (2003), 1526 (2004), 1617 (2005), 1735 (2006) and 1822 (2008).

On 28 April 2004, the Security Council adopted resolution 1540 (2004) under Chapter VII of the Charter of the United Nations, obliging States, inter alia, to refrain from supporting by any means non-State actors that attempt to develop, acquire, manufacture, possess, transport, transfer or use nuclear, chemical or biological weapons and their delivery systems. In resolution 1540 (2004) the Council imposed binding obligations on all States to establish domestic controls to prevent the proliferation of nuclear, chemical and biological weapons and their means of delivery, including by establishing appropriate controls over related materials.

In summary, the legal regime created by the universal instruments and relevant Security Council resolutions on counter-terrorism offers a wide array of criminal justice tools to address serious crimes committed by terrorists. It is based on the premise that perpetrators of terrorist crimes should be brought to trial by their national Governments or should be extradited to a country willing to bring them to trial. The well-known principle of *aut dedere, aut judicare* (extradite or prosecute) is meant to make the world inhospitable to terrorists (and those who finance and support them) by denying them safe havens. The regime also provides the legal framework for terrorism prevention through deterrence and a context for pursuing other prevention measures in conformity with the rule of law.

B. Importance of international cooperation

Effective international cooperation constitutes the cornerstone of a criminal justice response to international terrorism. As there are no international tribunals with competence to try acts of international terrorism as defined in the universal legal instruments, the duty to bring perpetrators of such criminal acts to justice rests solely with domestic courts. And because counter-terrorism operations, by nature, are often transnational in character and scope, they require investigators and prosecutors to work closely with their counterparts in other countries to gather evidence across borders.

The international community has come to recognize how hindered domestic authorities are when they confront criminals and terrorists who conduct their illegal activities in situations in which national borders serve as insulation from investigation and prosecution. The universal instruments against terrorism provide essential tools for extradition and mutual legal assistance that enable national authorities to cooperate with each other to ensure that there are no safe havens for terrorist suspects protecting them from prosecution and extradition.

The Security Council, in its resolution 1373 (2001) called upon States to increase cooperation and fully implement the relevant international conventions and protocols (para. 3 *(e)*) and decided that States shall deny safe haven to those who finance, plan, support or commit terrorist acts, or provide safe havens (para. 2 *(c)*). The resolution also requires States to afford one another the greatest measure of assistance in connection with criminal investigations or criminal proceedings relating to the financing or support of terrorist acts, including assistance in obtaining evidence in their possession necessary for proceedings (para. 2 *(f)*).

Indeed, the need for international cooperation in the fight against terrorism has been reiterated in numerous international instruments and declarations. The United Nations Global Counter-Terrorism Strategy enumerates the many levels on which that cooperation must take place and highlights the various commitments of Member States in working together to combat terrorism. The Strategy expresses the international community's resolve to cooperate fully in the fight against terrorism, in accordance with its obligations under international law, in order to find, deny safe haven and bring to justice, on the basis of the principle of extradite or prosecute, any person who supports, facilitates, participates or attempts to participate in the financing, planning, preparation or perpetration of terrorist acts or provides safe havens. In the Strategy, Member States resolve to undertake the following measures:

- To ensure the apprehension and prosecution or extradition of perpetrators of terrorist acts, in accordance with the relevant provisions of national and international law, in particular human rights law, refugee law and international humanitarian law;

- To conclude and implement mutual judicial assistance and extradition agreements and to strengthen cooperation between law enforcement agencies;

- To intensify cooperation, as appropriate, in exchanging timely and accurate information concerning the prevention and combating of terrorism;

- To strengthen coordination and cooperation among States in combating crimes that might be connected with terrorism, including drug trafficking in all its aspects, illicit arms trade, in particular of small arms and light weapons, including man-portable air defence systems, money-laundering and smuggling of nuclear, chemical, biological, radiological and other potentially deadly materials;

- To consider becoming parties without delay to the United Nations Convention against Transnational Organized Crime and the Protocols thereto,[22] and implementing them;

- To take appropriate measures, before granting asylum, for the purpose of ensuring that the asylum-seeker has not engaged in terrorist activities and, after granting asylum, for the purpose of ensuring that the refugee status is not abused;

- To encourage relevant regional and subregional organizations to create or strengthen counter-terrorism mechanisms or centres;

- To step up national efforts and bilateral, subregional, regional and international cooperation, as appropriate, to improve border and customs controls.

All these measures require a sufficient criminal justice capacity to engage in various forms of international cooperation in a way that complies with new international standards. Developing such a capacity may involve legal reforms, the introduction of complex procedural reforms and, generally, the development of a much greater investigation and prosecution capacity at the national level as well as the strengthening of the capacity to cooperate at the international level.

International cooperation mechanisms

The main mechanisms supporting international cooperation are mutual legal assistance, extradition, transfer of prisoners, transfer of proceedings in criminal matters, international

---

[22]United Nations, *Treaty Series*, vols. 2225, 2237, 2241 and 2326, No. 39574.

cooperation for the purposes of confiscation of criminal proceeds and asset recovery. These mechanisms, while essentially governed by domestic law, are supported by regional or international agreements or arrangements, including the universal legal instruments against terrorism, the Organized Crime Convention and the United Nations Convention against Corruption.[23] All these mechanisms are evolving rapidly to keep pace with new technologies. That evolution reflects the new determination of Member States to work more closely with each other to face the growing threats of organized crime, corruption and terrorism.[24]

Having national legislation in place to fully implement these instruments is therefore of paramount importance for the fight against terrorist crimes, as are the development of a capacity to cooperate and the implementation of the administrative measures necessary to support the various modalities of international cooperation. UNODC has developed useful tools to assist Member States in this regard, including the manual for international cooperation in criminal matters against terrorism.

The question of international cooperation, as it relates to each component of the criminal justice system, will be further addressed in part two of the *Handbook*.

C. International human rights law

Terrorism has a serious impact on human rights, with grave consequences for the enjoyment of the right to life, liberty and the physical integrity of victims and their families. It can also weaken social institutions, threaten economic development, fuel conflicts and thus affect the rights of all citizens in countless ways.

Terrorism therefore needs to be countered with all the legitimate means at the disposal of the State. Yet, counter-terrorism measures that ignore or damage human rights are self-defeating and unacceptable in a society guided by the rule of law and democratic values. Human rights are universal values and legal guarantees that protect individuals and groups against actions and omissions, caused primarily by State action, that interfere with fundamental freedoms, entitlements and human dignity. Human rights are universal, interdependent and indivisible. Counter-terrorism efforts and enforceable human rights standards are not only compatible; they are mutually reinforcing.

"Upholding human rights is not at odds with battling terrorism: on the contrary, the moral vision of human rights—the deep respect for the dignity of each person—is among our most powerful weapons against it."

Former Secretary-General
Kofi Annan, September 2003

The Universal Declaration of Human Rights[25] is built on the fundamental principle that human rights are based on the "inherent dignity ... of all members of the human family" and are the "foundation of freedom, justice and peace in the world". Security of the individual is a basic human right and, accordingly, the protection of individuals is a fundamental obligation of Governments. Article 3 of the Declaration states that "Everyone

---

[23] Ibid., vol. 2349, No. 42146.

[24] See also M. Joutsen, "The Evolution of Cooperation in Criminal Matters within the European Union: the Record so Far", in K. Aromaa and T. Viljanen (eds.), *International Key Issues in Crime Prevention and Criminal Justice* (Helsinki, HEUNI, 2006), pp. 67-91.

[25] General Assembly resolution 217 A (III).

has the right to life, liberty and security of person". The International Covenant on Civil and Political Rights[26] provides, in its article 6, that "Every human being has the inherent right to life. This right shall be protected by law. No one shall be arbitrarily deprived of his life."

United Nations core human rights treaties

- International Convention on the Elimination of All Forms of Racial Discrimination

- International Covenant on Economic, Social and Cultural Rights

- International Covenant on Civil and Political Rights and its two Optional Protocols

- Convention against Torture and Other Cruel, Inhuman or Degrading Treatment or Punishment

- Convention on the Rights of the Child and its two Optional Protocols

- International Convention on the Protection of the Rights of All Migrant Workers and Members of Their Families

- Convention on the Elimination of All Forms of Discrimination against Women and its Optional Protocol

- International Convention for the Protection of All Persons from Enforced Disappearance

There is also a growing body of subject-specific treaties and protocols, as well as various regional treaties on the protection of human rights and fundamental freedoms.

Complying with these obligations requires States to develop national counter-terrorism strategies that seek to prevent terrorism and prosecute and punish those responsible for terrorist acts in a manner that is consistent with the promotion of and respect for human rights. Such strategies must also include measures to prevent the spread of terrorism, including measures to reinforce human rights, prevent ethnic, national or religious discrimination, political exclusion and socio-economic marginalization, as well as measures to address impunity for human rights violations.

International human rights instruments

The two principal instruments deriving from the Universal Declaration of Human Rights are the International Covenant on Civil and Political Rights and the International Covenant on Economic, Social and Cultural Rights.[27] The two covenants were adopted in 1966 and entered into force in 1976.

The Universal Declaration of Human Rights has inspired a number of other human rights conventions. They include conventions to prevent and prohibit specific abuses such as racism (the International Convention on the Elimination of All Forms of Racial Discrimination[28]) and torture (the Convention against Torture and Other Cruel, Inhuman or Degrading Treatment or Punishment[29]). Other instruments have been adopted to protect especially vulnerable populations or classes of persons, such as the Convention relating to the Status of Refugees.[30]

---

[26]United Nations, *Treaty Series*, vol. 999, No. 14668.

[27]General Assembly resolution 2200 A (XXI), annex.

[28]United Nations, *Treaty Series*, vol. 660, No. 9464.

[29]Ibid., vol. 1465, No. 24841.

[30]Ibid., vol. 189, No. 2545.

The International Covenant on Civil and Political Rights details the basic civil and political rights of individuals, and duties attached to the State, including the following:

* The right to life;
* The right to liberty and freedom of movement;
* The right to equality before the law;
* The right to presumption of innocence until proven guilty;
* The right to be recognized as a person before the law;
* The right to privacy and protection of that privacy by law;
* The right to legal recourse when rights are violated;
* Freedom of thought, conscience and religion or belief;
* Freedom of opinion and expression;
* Freedom of assembly and association.

The Covenant forbids torture and inhuman or degrading treatment, slavery, arbitrary arrest and detention and propaganda advocating either war or hatred based on race, religion, national origin or language. It prohibits discrimination on any basis, such as race, sex, colour, national origin or language.

In the case of human rights treaties, States parties to a particular treaty have obligations under that treaty. However, international human rights law is not limited to the enumeration of rights within treaties. It also includes rights and freedoms that have become part of customary international law, which means that they bind all States, whether or not they are party to a particular treaty. For example, many of the rights set out in the Universal Declaration of Human Rights, as well as some of the rights defined in the International Covenant on Civil and Political Rights, reflect norms of customary international law. Customary international law is an important source of law. It is particularly relevant as it relates to human rights law as well as counter-terrorism. It consists of

> rules of law derived from the consistent conduct of States acting out of the belief that the law required them to act that way. It results from a general and consistent practice of States followed out of a sense of legal obligation, so much so that it becomes custom. Customary international law must be derived from a clear consensus among States as exhibited both by widespread conduct and a discernible sense of obligation.[31]

The notion of *ius cogens* refers to particular elements of customary international law based on a principle of international law that are so fundamental that no State may opt out by way of treaty or otherwise. In other words, they are regarded as being peremptory in nature and as enjoying a non-derogable character. The prohibitions against torture, slavery, genocide, racial discrimination and crimes against humanity are widely recognized as peremptory norms.

The adoption of many human rights instruments has led to the establishment of special monitoring bodies with a mandate to receive and investigate complaints of violations of individual rights and to adjudicate or at least report on them. For instance, a Special Rapporteur on the promotion and protection of human rights and fundamental freedoms

---

[31]Organization for Security and Cooperation in Europe, Office for Democratic Institutions and Human Rights, *Countering Terrorism, Protecting Human Rights: a Manual* (Warsaw, ODIHR, 2007), p. 55.

while countering terrorism was given a mandate under the Human Rights Council to investigate and report on the causes and consequences of violations of human rights in relation to counter-terrorism measures. National and regional mechanisms have also been established to respond to alleged violations.

A number of the guarantees contained in the International Covenant on Civil and Political Rights and other human rights treaties relate, in one way or another, to counter-terrorism measures. Ensuring both the protection of human rights and the effective use of counter-terrorism measures often raises some practical challenges. Several of those challenges as they relate to the criminal justice system are considered in part three of the present *Handbook*. There is, however, enough flexibility within the international human rights legal framework to deal with those complex issues. For example, in exceptional circumstances, a State may lawfully impose some restrictions upon the enjoyment of certain human rights. Human rights law creates a possibility of recourse to limitations in relation to certain rights and, in a very limited set of circumstances, of derogating from certain human rights provisions.

Limitations to the exercise of human rights

States may legitimately limit the exercise of certain rights. For example, when necessary in a democratic society, the exercise of freedom of expression, freedom of association or freedom of assembly may be legitimately limited by a State in the pursuit of a legitimate purpose, as long as that limitation respects certain conditions. The right to liberty is another example of a limited right. The right is asserted in the International Covenant on Civil and Political Rights in a way that also spells out specific limits that may apply. The principles of necessity and proportionality must be respected.

The permissible legitimate purposes for limiting the exercise of certain rights may include national security, public safety, public order, health, morals and the human rights and freedoms of others. In cases involving terrorist threats, public safety and/or national security are the purposes most likely to be invoked to justify measures limiting certain rights.

Moreover, in some exceptional circumstances, such as an emergency that threatens the life of the nation, a State may take measures that derogate from certain human rights provisions under the International Covenant on Civil and Political Rights. The conditions under which a legitimate temporary derogation from certain obligations under the Covenant is possible are defined in article 4, paragraph 1, of the Covenant:

> In time of public emergency which threatens the life of the nation and the existence of which is officially proclaimed, the States Parties to the present Covenant may take measures derogating from their obligations under the present Covenant to the extent strictly required by the exigencies of the situation, provided that such measures are not inconsistent with their other obligations under international law and do not involve discrimination solely on the ground of race, colour, sex, language, religion or social origin.

Under the Covenant, the mere presence of a terrorist threat does not necessarily constitute a "public emergency". Emergencies must therefore be assessed on a case-by-case basis. The provisions of the Covenant allowing for certain derogations in a public emergency are to be interpreted restrictively. The derogation is an authorized and limited prerogative of a State in order to allow it to respond adequately to a threat to the life of the nation. The derogating State must still justify its actions under law.

Threat to the life of the nation[a]

39. A State party may take measures derogating from its obligations under the International Covenant on Civil and Political Rights pursuant to article 4 (hereinafter called "derogation measures") only when faced with a situation of exceptional and actual or imminent danger which threatens the life of the nation. A threat to the life of the nation is one that:

(a) Affects the whole of the population and either the whole or part of the territory of the State, and

(b) Threatens the physical integrity of the population, the political independence or the territorial integrity of the State or the existence or basic functioning of institutions indispensable to ensure and project the rights recognized in the Covenant.

40. Internal conflict and unrest that do not constitute a grave and imminent threat to the life of the nation cannot justify derogations under article 4.

41. Economic difficulties per se cannot justify derogation measures.

[a]Siracusa Principles on the Limitation and Derogation Provisions in the International Covenant on Civil and Political Rights (E/CN.4/1985/4, annex, paras. 39-41).

Any derogation under article 4, paragraph 1, of the Covenant must be necessary and proportional. As stated in article 4, any derogation of rights in times of emergency may be only "to the extent strictly required by the exigencies of the situation". Key to that requirement is the temporary nature of any derogation and the obligation of States to restore normalcy as quickly as possible.

Establishing the necessity of the derogation[a]

51. The severity, duration, and geographic scope of any derogation measure shall be such only as are strictly necessary to deal with the threat to the life of the nation and are proportionate to its nature and extent.

52. The competent national authorities shall have a duty to assess individually the necessity of any derogation measure taken or proposed to deal with the specific dangers posed by the emergency.

53. A measure is not strictly required by the exigencies of the situation where ordinary measures permissible under the specific limitations clauses of the Covenant would be adequate to deal with the threat to the life of the nation.

54. The principle of strict necessity shall be applied in an objective manner. Each measure shall be directed to an actual, clear, present or imminent danger and may not be imposed merely because of an apprehension of potential danger.

55. The national constitution and laws governing states of emergency shall provide for prompt and periodic independent review by the legislature of the necessity for derogation measures.

56. Effective remedies shall be available to persons claiming that derogation measures affecting them are not strictly required by the exigencies of the situation.

57. In determining whether derogation measures are strictly required by the exigencies of the situation, the judgement of the national authorities cannot be accepted as conclusive.

[a]Siracusa Principles on the Limitation and Derogation Provisions in the International Covenant on Civil and Political Rights (E/CN.4/1985/4, annex, paras. 51-57).

A State party derogating from its obligations under the Covenant must make an official proclamation of the existence of the public emergency threatening the life of the nation and immediately notify other States parties to the Covenant. Procedures should exist under national law for the proclamation of a state of emergency.

However, there are certain human rights set out in international treaties that cannot be derogated from, not even in situations of a "public emergency which threatens the life of the nation". Article 4, paragraph 2, of the Covenant identifies the following non-derogable rights: the right to life; the prohibition of torture or cruel, inhuman or degrading treatment or punishment; the prohibition against slavery and servitude; freedom from imprisonment for failure to fulfil a contract; freedom from retrospective penalties; the right to be recognized as a person before the law; and freedom of thought, conscience and religion.

Non-derogable rights guaranteed by the International Covenant on Civil and Political Rights

The International Covenant on Civil and Political Rights guarantees that are not subject to derogation, even in an emergency threatening the life of the nation, are contained in the following articles:

Article 6

Every human being has the inherent right to life. This right shall be protected by law. No one shall be arbitrarily deprived of his life.

Article 7

No one shall be subjected to torture or to cruel, inhuman or degrading treatment or punishment.

Article 8

No one shall be held in slavery; slavery and the slave-trade in all their forms shall be prohibited. No one shall be held in servitude. No one shall be required to perform forced or compulsory labour.

Article 11

No one shall be imprisoned merely on the ground of inability to fulfil a contractual obligation.

Article 15

No one shall be held guilty of any criminal offence on account of any act or omission which did not constitute a criminal offence, under national or international law, at the time when it was committed.

Article 16

Everyone shall have the right to recognition everywhere as a person before the law.

Article 18

Everyone shall have the right to freedom of thought, conscience and religion. Freedom to manifest one's religion or beliefs may be subject only to such limitations as are prescribed by law and are necessary to protect public safety, order, health, or morals or the fundamental rights and freedoms of others.

The Human Rights Committee of the Office of the United Nations High Commissioner for Human Rights has also identified rights and freedoms under customary international law that may not be derogated from, including the following:

- The right of all persons deprived of their liberty to be treated with humanity and with respect for the inherent dignity of the human person;

- The prohibitions against abductions and unacknowledged detentions; the international protection of the rights of persons belonging to minorities;

- The deportation or forcible transfer of populations without grounds recognized under international law; the prohibition against taking hostages;

- The prohibition against propaganda for war or in advocacy of national, racial or religious hatred that would constitute an incitement to discrimination, hostility or violence.

Protection against "refoulement"

In its resolution 60/158 of 16 December 2005, the General Assembly reaffirmed the obligation of States, in accordance with article 4 of the International Covenant on Civil and Political Rights, to respect certain rights as non-derogable in any circumstances. The Assembly recalled, in regard to all other Covenant rights, that any measures derogating from the provisions of the Covenant must be in accordance with that article in all cases, and underlined the exceptional and temporary nature of any such derogations. The Assembly called upon States to raise awareness about the importance of these obligations among national authorities involved in combating terrorism.

The principle of non-refoulement, found in article 3 of the Convention against Torture and Other Cruel, Inhuman or Degrading Treatment or Punishment, prohibits the expulsion of a person to States where there are substantial grounds for believing he would be at risk of torture or other serious human rights violations. The principle, when it is respected, offers very important human rights protection in the counter-terrorism context. The same principle was already contained in the 1951 Convention relating to the Status of Refugees, signed at Geneva on 28 July 1951, which, in its article 33, prohibited contracting States from expelling or returning ("refouler") refugees to the frontiers of territories where their life or freedom would be threatened on account of their race, religion, nationality, membership of a particular social group or political opinion.

Article 3, on non-refoulement, of the Convention against Torture

1.   No State Party shall expel, return ("refouler") or extradite a person to another State where there are substantial grounds for believing that he would be in danger of being subjected to torture.

2.   For the purpose of determining whether there are such grounds, the competent authorities shall take into account all relevant considerations including, where applicable, the existence in the State concerned of a consistent pattern of gross, flagrant or mass violations of human rights.

In its resolution 60/158, the General Assembly also urged States to fully respect non-refoulement obligations under international refugee and human rights law and, at the same time, to review, with full respect for those obligations and other legal safeguards, the validity of a refugee status decision in an individual case if credible and relevant evidence comes to light that indicates that the person in question has committed any criminal acts, including terrorist acts, falling under the exclusion clauses under international refugee law.

Discrimination

Article 1 of the Charter of the United Nations states that one of the purposes of the United Nations is to achieve international cooperation in promoting and encouraging respect for human rights and for fundamental freedoms for all without distinction as to race, sex, language or religion. Principles of equality and non-discrimination are essential to combating and preventing terrorism. The need to counter terrorism should not become a pretext for allowing discrimination and intolerance to flourish.

Care must be taken to ensure that counter-terrorism measures do not amount to a form of discrimination. The Committee on the Elimination of Racial Discrimination of the Office of the United Nations High Commissioner for Human Rights has issued a statement recalling that the prohibition of racial discrimination is a peremptory norm of international law from which no derogation is permitted, and requesting States and international organizations to ensure that counter-terrorism measures do not discriminate, in purpose or effect, on grounds of race, colour, descent or national or ethnic origin.

A 2004 recommendation by the Council of Europe's European Commission against Racism and Intolerance on combating racism while fighting terrorism[32] provides guidance on the steps to be taken to ensure that counter-terrorism measures are not discriminatory. The guidelines recommend that States ensure that no discrimination ensues from legislation, regulations, policies or practices concerning the following:

- Checks carried out by law-enforcement officials and border control personnel;
- Administrative and pretrial detention;
- Conditions of detention;
- Fair trial, criminal procedure;
- Protection of personal data;
- Protection of private and family life;
- Expulsion, extradition, deportation and the principle of non-refoulement;
- Issuance of visas;
- Residence and work permits and family reunification;
- Acquisition and revocation of citizenship.

D.   International refugee law

International refugee law provides a legal framework for the protection of refugees. It defines the term "refugee", sets out States' obligations concerning refugees and establishes standards for their treatment. It also covers the situation of persons seeking asylum. The two universal instruments establishing that framework are the Convention Relating to the Status of Refugees of 1951 and the 1967 Protocol Relating to the Status of Refugees.[33]

In 2001, the Office of the United Nations High Commissioner for Refugees (UNHCR) issued a statement containing the following observation:

> Any discussion on security safeguards should start from the assumption that refugees are themselves escaping persecution and violence, including terrorist acts, and are not the perpetrators of such acts. Another starting point is that the international refugee instruments do not provide a safe haven to terrorists and do not protect them from criminal prosecution. On the contrary, they render the identification of persons engaged in terrorist activities possible and necessary, foresee their exclusion from refugee status and do not shield them against either criminal prosecution or expulsion.[34]

---

[32]European Commission against Racism and Intolerance General Policy Recommendation No. 8, on combating racism while fighting terrorism, adopted on 17 March 2004.

[33]United Nations, *Treaty Series*, vol. 606, No. 8791.

[34]Office of the United Nations High Commissioner for Refugees, "Addressing security concerns without undermining refugee protection: UNHCR's perspective", statement issued on 29 November 2001; available at www.unhcr.org/refworld/docid/3c0b880e0.html.

There should be no avenue for terrorists to secure access to territory, whether to find a safe haven, avoid prosecution or to carry out further attacks. Security Council resolution 1373 (2001) touches upon a number of issues related to immigration and refugee status. States are required to prevent the movement of terrorists by implementing effective border controls and to take measures to secure the integrity of identity papers and travel documents (para. 2 *(g)*). States are also called upon to take measures to ensure that refugee status is not granted to asylum seekers who have planned, facilitated or participated in terrorist acts (para. 3 *(f)*) and to ensure that refugee status is not abused by perpetrators, organizers or facilitators of terrorist acts.

Those requirements do not create new obligations under international refugee law. They simply recognize that appropriate mechanisms need to be put in place in the field of asylum, as they have been in other fields. At the same time, care should be taken to ensure a proper balance with the principles of refugee protection. All persons have a right to seek asylum. Public safety and security measures should not have the effect of criminalizing refugees. The Convention relating to the Status of Refugees, when properly implemented, is sufficient to ensure that international refugee protection is not extended to those who have induced, facilitated or perpetrated serious crimes, a category that includes terrorist acts.

Grounds for exclusion from international refugee protection

According to article 1F of the Convention relating to the Status of Refugees, persons who would otherwise meet the refugee criteria set by the Convention shall be excluded from international refugee protection if there are serious reasons for considering that they have committed a war crime, a crime against humanity, a serious non-political crime outside the country of refuge prior to admission to that country as a refugee, or have been guilty of acts contrary to the purposes and principles of the United Nations. International refugee law requires an assessment of the context and circumstances of the individual case through a fair and efficient procedure before a decision is taken. UNHCR has issued guidelines on the application of exclusion clauses under the Convention.[35]

Asylum seekers and terrorists

"Equating asylum with a safe haven for terrorists is not only legally wrong and thus far unsupported by facts, but it serves to vilify refugees in the public mind and promotes the singling out of persons of particular races or religions for discrimination and hate-based harassment.

"Since 11 September, a number of immigrant and refugee communities have suffered attacks and harassment based on perceived ethnicity or religion, heightening social tensions. While there are some asylum-seekers and refugees who have been, or will be, associated with serious crime, this does not mean that the majority should be damned by association with the few."

UNHCR, "Addressing Security Concerns without
Undermining Refugee Protection–UNHCR's Perspective",
29 November 2001.

---

[35]UNHCR Guidelines on International Protection: Application of the Exclusion Clauses: Article 1F of the 1951 Convention relating to the Status of Refugees (HCR/GIP/03/05).

The summary rejection of asylum-seekers at borders or points of entry is not permitted. Each claim, even where there is a suspicion of involvement in serious criminal acts, should be determined on its own merits and not based on negative and discriminatory presumptions deriving from the nationality, ethnic origin or religious faith of the claimant. It should be noted also that article 33, paragraph 2, of the Convention relating to the Status of Refugees provides for possible exceptions to the principle of non-refoulement. Denial of protection from refoulement and return to the country of origin is foreseen in cases where there are reasonable grounds for regarding a refugee as a danger to the security of the country in which he or she is, or if a refugee who has been convicted of a particularly serious crime constitutes a danger to the community of the host State.

Since issues of exclusion can be complicated, UNHCR advocates that they should continue to be dealt with through the regular asylum procedure, which allows for a full factual and legal assessment of the individual case by qualified personnel. According to UNHCR:

> Non-admission at borders and barring access to the asylum procedure not only endangers bona fide asylum-seekers but could serve, ironically, as an incentive to terrorism by encouraging those involved to seek entry through illegal means, thereby removing the possibility of identification through the interview process accompanying asylum adjudications.[34]

Finally, when a person has already been granted refugee status, that status may be cancelled where there are grounds for considering that the person should not have been granted such a status at the time of the decision. For instance, the individual may not have met the inclusion criteria at the time that the decision was made, or an exclusion clause of the Convention should have been applied; this can obviously include evidence that the person was involved in a terrorist conspiracy.

Expulsion of refugees

Expulsion and exclusion are two different processes. Excluded persons do not deserve international refugee protection. They are excluded from refugee status because of the severity of crimes that they have committed in the past. It protects the institution of asylum from abuse. Expulsion is a different matter: it deals with the danger that a refugee may constitute to the country of refuge.

International law, in particular articles 32 and 33, paragraph 2, of the Convention relating to the Status of Refugees provide for the expulsion of recognized refugees on "grounds of national security or public order". Expulsion aims to protect the country of refuge and hinges on the appreciation of a present or future threat. However, expulsion or return ("refoulement") of refugees in any manner whatsoever to the frontiers of territories where their life or freedom would be threatened on account of race, religion, nationality, membership of a particular social group or political opinion is not permitted under the Convention (art. 33, para. 1).

UNHCR has expressed a concern that States may be inclined to expel groups or individuals based on religious, ethnic or national origin, or political affiliation, on the mere assumption that they may be involved in terrorism. Expulsion decisions must be reached in accordance with a due process of law that substantiates the security threat and allows the individual to provide any evidence that might counter the allegations. Article 32, paragraph 2, of the Convention states that "except where compelling reasons of national security otherwise require, the refugee shall be allowed to submit evidence to clear himself, and to appeal to and be represented for the purpose before competent authority or a person or persons specially designated by the competent authority".

E. International humanitarian law

International humanitarian law, also known as the "law of war" and the "law of armed conflict", is a set of rules seeking to protect persons who are not—or are no longer—participating in the hostilities and to restrict the means and methods of warfare. Humanitarian law covers three fundamental aspects of armed conflicts: separating legal military operations from illegal ones, protecting civilians during armed conflict and regulating the weaponry of armed conflict.

The principal sources of international humanitarian law are the following:

- The four Geneva Conventions of 1949;[36]
- The two additional Protocols to the Geneva Conventions, of 1977;[37]
- A number of treaties prohibiting or restricting the use of specific weapons, such as the Convention on Certain Conventional Weapons[38] and the Protocols thereto;
- The Convention for the Protection of Cultural Property in the Event of Armed Conflict;[39]
- Instruments establishing international mechanisms for the enforcement of international humanitarian law, such as the Rome Statute of the International Criminal Court;[40]
- An important body of customary law.

There is no explicit definition of "terrorism" as a crime in international humanitarian law, but that body of law prohibits certain acts committed in armed conflicts that are similar to terrorist acts as defined by the universal legal instruments against terrorism and that would be covered by these latter instruments if they were committed in times of peace. The taking of hostages is, for example, not only considered an offence under the International Convention against the Taking of Hostages,[41] but is also prohibited by common article 3 of the Geneva Conventions, which concerns persons taking no active part in hostilities in the case of an armed conflict not of an international character, and by article 34 of the Fourth Geneva Convention, which concerns individuals who in the case of a conflict of an international character or occupation, find themselves in the hands of a party to the conflict or Occupying Power of which they are not nationals, as well as being prohibited by the two Additional Protocols to the Geneva Conventions.[42]

It should be noted that the two Additional Protocols to the Geneva Conventions specifically prohibit acts or threats of violence the primary purpose of which is to spread terror among the civilian population.[43]

---

[36]United Nations, *Treaty Series*, vol. 75, Nos. 970-973.

[37]United Nations, *Treaty Series*, vol. 1125, Nos. 17512 and 17513.

[38]Convention on Prohibitions or Restrictions on the Use of Certain Conventional Weapons Which May Be Deemed to Be Excessively Injurious or to Have Indiscriminate Effects (United Nations, *Treaty Series*, vol. 1342, No. 22495).

[39]United Nations, *Treaty Series*, vol. 249, No. 3511.

[40]United Nations, *Treaty Series*, vol. 2187, No. 38544.

[41]United Nations, *Treaty Series*, vol. 1316, No. 21931.

[42]Protocol Additional to the Geneva Conventions of 12 August 1949, and relating to the Protection of Victims of International Armed Conflicts (Protocol I) of 8 June 1977, art. 75, para. 2 *(c)*; and Protocol Additional to the Geneva Conventions of 12 August 1949, and relating to the Protection of Victims of Non-International Armed Conflicts (Protocol II) of 8 June 1977, art. 4, para. 2 *(c)*.

[43]Protocol I, art. 51, para. 2; Protocol II, art. 13, para. 2.

Many of the international conventions and protocols related to the prevention and suppression of terrorism contain clauses of exception in relation to the military and times of war, stating that activities of armed forces during an armed conflict, governed by international humanitarian law, are not governed by the conventions. Article 19, paragraph 2, of the International Convention for the Suppression of Terrorist Bombings,[44] for example, states the following:

> The activities of armed forces during an armed conflict, as those terms are understood under international humanitarian law, which are governed by that law, are not governed by this Convention, and the activities undertaken by military forces of a State in the exercise of their official duties, inasmuch as they are governed by other rules of international law, are not governed by this Convention.

It should be understood that the application of international humanitarian law does not in any way prevent or obstruct a criminal justice response to terrorist acts, including the criminalization of incitement, conspiracy and the financing of terrorist acts. It does not prevent offenders from being held accountable by the criminal justice system. The International Committee of the Red Cross has frequently reaffirmed that compliance with international humanitarian law is in no manner an obstacle to the struggle against terrorism. In fact, full respect for international humanitarian law in counter-terrorism activities is a positive contribution to the eradication of terrorism.

F. Terrorism and transnational organized crime

Other elements of international law, in particular treaty-based criminal law, can be immediately relevant to the capacity of criminal justice systems to fight and prevent terrorism. An example of such treaty-based criminal law is the Organized Crime Convention. The main purpose of these treaties is to facilitate international cooperation in fighting various forms of transnational crime. States that have become parties to these treaties have undertaken to criminalize certain conduct and to develop the capacity of their respective criminal justice systems to work together to combat such crimes more effectively.

In paragraph 4 of its resolution 1373 (2001), the Security Council noted with concern the close connection between international terrorism and transnational organized crime, illicit drugs, money-laundering, illegal arms-trafficking, and illegal movement of nuclear, chemical, biological and other potentially deadly materials. That and other political statements referred to the possibility that alliances and various types of complicity and collaboration existed or might be formed between terrorist groups and conventional criminal organizations. Some have argued that those fears are exaggerated, while others claim that the threat is very real. The debate has received a considerable amount of attention both within and outside the United Nations.

Notwithstanding the debate about the nature of the link between organized crime and terrorism, it has become quite clear that Member States believe that they can strengthen their actions against terrorism by focusing their attention on other forms of criminal activity that precede or accompany terrorist crimes.

---

[44]United Nations, *Treaty Series*, vol. 2149, No. 37517.

There are, at minimum, two ways in which terrorists tend to be instrumentally involved in common criminality. First, in the absence of other financial means, terrorists become involved in various forms of lucrative conventional crimes, acquisitive or predatory, in order to support themselves and finance their main activities. Second, in the absence of normal access to some of the means that they require to conduct their terrorist activities, terrorists become involved in various crimes in order to procure such means. Various forms of human exploitation and conventional crime, including participating in and exploiting various illicit markets, become prerequisites for the conduct of successful terrorist operations.

Those are some of the reasons why it is increasingly important to try to better understand the manner in which terrorist organizations support their activities through the commission of other crimes. Ultimately, the objective is to develop strategies to prevent and disrupt such criminal activities in order to prevent terrorism.

In building the capacity of their own criminal justice systems to combat terrorism, States must keep in mind that terrorist groups are frequently involved in various forms of crime and that their conspiracies can sometimes be thwarted and effectively disrupted by focusing on related criminal activities. Furthermore, it does not make much sense for a State to attempt to build the capacity of its justice system to fight terrorism while ignoring the many other major challenges, including transnational organized crime and corruption, that these same systems must address at the same time.

One should note that many of the proven methods and strategies for combating organized crime are also relevant to the fight against terrorism. That makes sense for the following reasons: the intent and purposes of terrorist groups are criminal in nature; terrorist acts are crimes; terrorist groups frequently engage in criminal activities that are not in themselves "terrorist" in nature but that are nevertheless essential to the success of their enterprises; and the methods that the two types of groups—terrorists and organized criminal groups—use to intimidate people and to obstruct justice are often indistinguishable from each other.

United Nations Convention against Transnational Organized Crime

The Organized Crime Convention, adopted by the General Assembly in its resolution 55/25 of 15 November 2000, is the main international instrument in the fight against transnational organized crime. It entered into force on 29 September 2003.

The Convention is supplemented by three Protocols, which target specific areas and manifestations of organized crime: the Protocol to Prevent, Suppress and Punish Trafficking in Persons, Especially Women and Children; the Protocol against the Smuggling of Migrants by Land, Sea and Air; and the Protocol against the Illicit Manufacturing of and Trafficking in Firearms, their Parts and Components and Ammunition. Countries must become parties to the Convention before they can become parties to any of the Protocols.

The main purpose of the Convention is to foster and enhance close international cooperation in order to tackle the issues addressed. States that ratify the Convention commit themselves to taking a series of measures against transnational organized crime, including the establishment of domestic criminal offences (participation in an organized criminal group, money-laundering, corruption and the obstruction of justice); the adoption of new and sweeping frameworks for extradition, mutual legal assistance and law enforcement cooperation; and the promotion of training and technical assistance for building or upgrading the necessary capacity of national authorities.

In that context, experts agree that full use should be made of all appropriate international instruments to prevent and prosecute terrorism-related crimes. In particular, Member States can consider availing themselves of the mutual legal assistance and extradition provisions of those instruments, and of the dispositions and the international cooperation regime established by the States parties to the Organized Crime Convention and the Convention against Corruption.

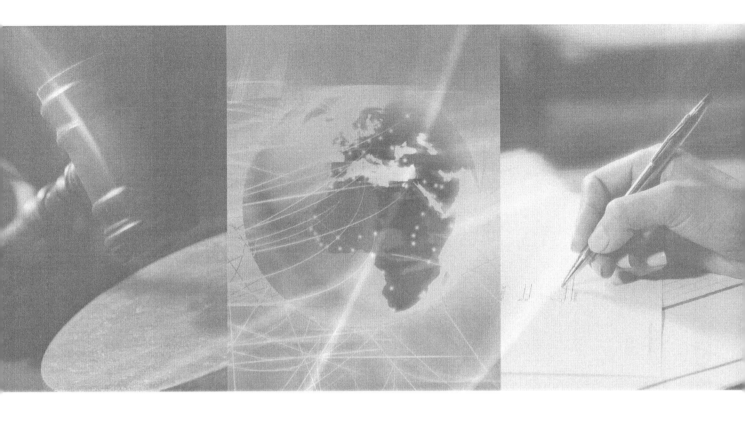

Part two
Key components of an effective criminal justice response to terrorism

I. Introduction

An effective rule of law-based criminal justice response to terrorism involves more than the mere ratification and implementation of the universal instruments against terrorism. In addition to the appropriate laws, policies and practices, criminal justice practitioners need ongoing capacity-building and specialized training to enable them to respond effectively to the increasingly complex nature of terrorist crimes.

Developing the capacity of a State's criminal justice system to respond to terrorism requires an approach that is integrated, coherent, sector-wide, human rights-based and sustainable. It is clear that an effective response to terrorism requires a justice system capable of functioning in an integrated fashion and relying on the strong contribution of all of its components, from the police, to the prosecution and defence bar, to the judiciary and the correctional system. States require a comprehensive capacity-building approach, which may involve law reform initiatives, increasing the overall capacity of justice institutions, increasing public credibility of these institutions and curbing corruption. Effective coordination horizontally, across the system, remains one of the essential preconditions to the success of any such initiative.[45]

Since its foundation, the United Nations has been active in the development and promotion of internationally recognized principles in crime prevention and criminal justice. Those standards and norms, which will be referred to extensively in the present guide, have contributed substantially to the promotion of more effective and fair criminal justice measures.[46] They can be utilized at the national level by fostering in-depth assessments leading to the adoption of necessary criminal justice reforms. They can help design national strategies for legal reform and for strengthening the rule of law. In effect, they also constitute best practices that can be adapted by States to meet national needs and reflect local circumstances. Part two of the *Handbook* considers some of the major challenges and issues faced by each component of a criminal justice system as part of the effort of responding to terrorism. It contains six chapters, dealing, respectively, with the issues and challenges encountered by policymakers and legislators, law enforcement agencies, legal counsel and the Bar, the prosecutors, the judiciary and the correctional systems. Applicable norms and standards are reviewed, and the adaptations of the system that may be necessitated by the special challenges associated with the prevention of terrorism are considered.

---

[45]M. Shaw and Y. Dandurand (eds.), *Maximizing the Effectiveness of the Technical Assistance Provided in the Fields of Crime Prevention and Criminal Justice* (Helsinki, HEUNI, 2006).

[46]See the *Compendium of United Nations Standards and Norms in Crime Prevention and Criminal Justice* (New York, 2006).

II. Role of policymakers and legislators

Policymakers and legislators must provide the policy and legal frameworks within which the criminal justice system exercises its counter-terrorism function. International law provides guidance for policy development and articulates the many obligations of States with respect to international cooperation, upholding the rule of law and protecting fundamental rights and freedoms.

This chapter of the *Handbook* examines the requirement for the legislative incorporation of international obligations, including the requirement to criminalize various types of conduct. It also refers to the need to periodically review legislation, together with its underlying policy framework, to ensure that they achieve their purposes with respect for the rule of law and human rights principles.

A. Legislative incorporation of international obligations

The rule of law requires that the laws of a State be comprehensive, clear, certain and accessible; they must be legitimate (legislatively and politically, as well as in their application), and they must balance stability and flexibility.

With respect to a State's formal obligations under the universal legal regime against terrorism, the State, following the ratification of the universal instruments, must proceed with their legislative incorporation based on a comprehensive review of its existing national law. This is necessary not only for the effective implementation of counter-terrorism measures but also for creating the legal basis to guide the work of criminal justice practitioners.

The process of becoming party to an international treaty or convention involves both an international and a domestic component. The international component consists of a formal procedure dictated by the terms of the agreement and governed by the principles of international law. An analysis of legislation is normally the first step to becoming a party to the global instruments against terrorism. That enables the Government and the legislature to anticipate the changes to their legal system that will be required as a result of membership of an international treaty or compliance with international standards.

Some States, because of domestic law or as a matter of policy, will not adopt a treaty until legislation is in place that permits the fulfilment of all its international obligations. The treaty has no domestic application until implemented by a domestic law. This is often referred to as the "dualist tradition", in which international law and domestic law are considered two separate systems. Legislation is required to introduce the international obligation into the domestic legal order.

In other countries—those that follow the monist tradition—once a treaty is ratified, it is automatically incorporated into domestic law. Under that system, some, if not most, of the provisions of the treaty become self-executing. However, even in those countries, legislation is often required to provide non-self-executing elements essential to the implementation of the treaty. The clearest example of this relates to the criminalization of various conducts as required by the global instruments against terrorism. None of those instruments specifies penalties for the offences in question. Domestic legislation is thus required.

Each State must opt for what it considers the most appropriate implementation mechanism. When the ratification of the pertinent universal instrument creates a binding obligation, the legal framework can be established by one of the following means:

- A comprehensive review of national criminal law and its relevant provisions, followed by amending legislation;

- The inclusion in a State's criminal law of a special section of its criminal code; sometimes, this a good option for a State that has the intention of undertaking broader reforms to its criminal law;

- The adoption of an autonomous law containing all the elements required by international conventions.

The third option may appear as the simplest and most attractive solution but may eventually lead to difficulties of implementation and interpretation if insufficient efforts are made to ensure that the new law is fully congruent with other national legislation.

The Terrorism Prevention Branch of UNODC has produced two guides for use by policymakers, legal drafters and legislators: the updated *Legislative Guide to the Universal Legal Regime against Terrorism*[47] and the *Guide for the Legislative Incorporation and Implementation of the Universal Anti-Terrorism Instruments.*[48] The Commonwealth Secretariat has also produced two useful tools to help policymakers plan the legislative implementation of the universal conventions against terrorism: the Model Legislative Provisions on Measures to Combat Terrorism and the Implementation Kits for the International Counter-Terrorism Conventions.

B. Criminalization

Effective criminalization of various acts associated with terrorist activities is a prerequisite to intervention by the criminal justice system. Criminalization is not only a legal obligation for States parties to the various instruments against terrorism but also a prerequisite for effective international cooperation. States parties are expected to establish under their domestic law a number of offences called for by the conventions and protocols relating to terrorism and other related forms of crime. They must also ensure that those offences are punishable by appropriate penalties that take into account the gravity of the offences. States must define the material and mental elements of the offences in accordance with their general criminal law. While doing so, they must also ensure that the new criminal law provisions comply with their other obligations under international law, in particular international human rights, refugee law and humanitarian law.

The universal instruments against terrorism require the criminalization of a certain number of acts in the areas that they regulate. The table below summarizes some of the offences that must be established under national law, if they do not already exist. The offences can be grouped into five categories: (1) offences related to civil aviation; (2) offences based

---

[47]United Nations publication, Sales No. E.08.V.9.

[48]Available at http://www.unodc.org/pdf/terrorism/TATs/en/2LIGen.pdf.

on the victim's status; (3) offences related to dangerous materials; (4) offences related to vessels, fixed platforms and harbour installations; and (5) offences related to the financing of terrorism. In addition, both the universal instruments against terrorism and Security Council resolution 1373 (2001) require the criminalization of certain ancillary offences relating to the planning and preparation of terrorist acts, as well as participation in those acts.

Examples of criminalization required under the universal instruments against terrorism

- Offences relating to civil aviation

- Offences based on the status of the victims (internationally protected persons and hostages)

- Offences related to dangerous materials, including plastic explosives, weapons of mass destruction as defined in the International Convention for the Suppression of Terrorist Bombings, and materials covered by the Convention on the Physical Protection of Nuclear Material (1979) and its 2005 Amendment and the International Convention for the Suppression of Acts of Nuclear Terrorism (2005)

- Offences related to vessels, fixed platforms and harbour installations

- Offences related to the financing of terrorism (also required by Security Council resolution 1373 (2001))

The issue of the extent of participation that gives rise to criminal liability in relation to terrorism is essential. The universal instruments require punishment of both the perpetrators and accomplices of completed or attempted offences and, for specific offences, persons who organize, direct or threaten to commit terrorist acts.

Relevance of the rule of law and human rights

In the definition of terrorist acts or terrorism-related crimes, States must observe the basic human rights principle of legality (*nullum crimen, nulla poena sine lege*), which requires precision and clarity when drafting laws and prohibits the ex post facto adoption of a law or the retroactive criminalization of a conduct. This principle of general inter-national law is enshrined and made expressly non-derogable in article 4 of the International Covenant on Civil and Political Rights and the provisions of regional human rights treaties. It prohibits not only the application of ex post facto laws, but also requires that the crimnalized conduct be described in precise and unambiguous language that narrowly defines the punishable offence and distinguishes it from conduct that is either not punishable or is punishable by other penalties. Accordingly, the principle of legality also entails the principle of certainty, which means that the law must be reasonably predictable in its application and consequences.

Criminalizing conspiracies and criminal associations

As mentioned earlier, it is important to be able to counter a terrorist conspiracy before it achieves its goals. If terrorist violence is to be reduced, authorities must be able to refocus their attention on proactive intervention at the planning and preparation stages. Criminalizing various preparatory conduct may facilitate early intervention, as can the creation of conspiracy or criminal association offences.

The offences of conspiracy and criminal association are obvious models for preventive intervention against the planning and preparation of criminal acts. Criminal responsibility at a time preceding actual violence can be established in law through the continental law concept of *association de malfaiteurs* and/or the common law concept of "conspiracy", both of which prohibit agreements to commit crime. For these offences to be complete, the intended harmful act need not be attempted or accomplished, although some laws require the commission of a preparatory step to carry out the group's purposes.

Criminalizing conspiracies to commit a terrorist act (even when the terrorist act has not yet been carried out), depending on the national law and the legal tradition, may raise all kinds of evidentiary difficulties. However, it is possible to criminalize financial preparations of terrorist acts, as now required of States parties to the International Convention for the Suppression of the Financing of Terrorism. This relatively new approach introduces a deliberate strategy to permit intervention before a terrorist atrocity has been committed or attempted. Instead of defining a violent offence that can be punished only if it succeeds or is attempted, article 2 of the Convention requires the criminalization of the non-violent financial preparations that precede nearly every terrorist attack.

One must remember that the right to freedom of association is central to a democratic society; it is a platform for the exercise and defence of other rights, such as political participation and cultural rights. It is true that the right to freedom of association may be subject to derogations and limitations under most human rights treaties. However, in addition to the respect of the principles of necessity and proportionality in limiting these rights, specific precautions are also important in order to ensure that the limitations in question are narrowly defined and are not used to limit the rights of legitimate opposition parties, trade unions or human rights defenders. Any decision to proscribe a group or association needs to be carried out on a case-by-case basis and must be subject to judicial oversight.

Criminalizing the financing of terrorism

Preventing terrorists and terrorist organizations from funding their activities and planned attacks is an essential component of any successful global counter-terrorism campaign. International efforts to combat transnational financial crime and terrorist financing have evolved considerably in recent years. During the 1990s, most of these efforts were spearheaded by a number of intergovernmental organizations, most notably the Financial Action Task Force (FATF), the FATF-style regional bodies and the International Monetary Fund.

Global efforts to combat terrorist financing were enhanced in 1999 through the International Convention for the Suppression of the Financing of Terrorism. Article 2, paragraph 1, of the Convention provides that "any person commits an offence within the meaning of this Convention if that person by any means, directly or indirectly, unlawfully and wilfully, provides or collects funds with the intention that they should be used or in the knowledge that they are to be used, in full or in part, in order to carry out [certain defined acts]".

According to the Convention's definition, the mens rea, or element of intention, behind the financing of terrorism has two aspects: the act must be committed wilfully and the offender must intend to use the funds to finance acts of terrorism or know that they will be used for that purpose.

The Convention also obliges States parties to hold legal persons liable under specific circumstances. Article 5 obliges each State party to take the necessary measures to enable a legal entity located in its territory or organized under its laws to be held liable when a person responsible for the management or control of that legal entity has, in that capacity, committed an offence as set forth in article 2. Such liability may be criminal, civil or administrative, although recent practice leans more towards establishing criminal corporate liability whenever possible.[49]

In the same vein, the Security Council, in paragraph 1 *(b)* of its resolution 1373 (1999), required States to criminalize the wilful provision or collection, by any means, directly or indirectly, of funds by their nationals or in their territories with the intention that the funds should be used, or in the knowledge that they are to be used, in order to carry out terrorist acts.

Incitement to terrorism

The Security Council, in its resolution 1624 (2005), called upon all States to adopt such measures as may be necessary and appropriate and in accordance with their obligations under international law to:

(a) Prohibit by law incitement to commit a terrorist act or acts;

(b) Prevent such conduct;

(c) Deny safe haven to any persons with respect to whom there is credible and relevant information giving serious reasons for considering that they have been guilty of such conduct.

In that resolution, the Security Council also called upon all States to continue international efforts to enhance dialogue and broaden understanding among civilizations, in an effort to prevent the indiscriminate targeting of different religions and cultures, and to take all measures as may be necessary and appropriate and in accordance with their obligations under international law to counter incitement of terrorist acts motivated by extremism and intolerance and to prevent the subversion of educational, cultural and religious institutions by terrorists and their supporters.

Because terrorist propaganda incites discrimination, hostility and violence by advocating hatred on national, racial or religious grounds, penalizing such incitement is a direct means of implementing the International Covenant on Civil and Political Rights, even when the harm being incited does not occur. Prohibiting such incitement based upon the additional grounds of cultural differences would seem to be an entirely consistent extension of the proactive, preventive approach reflected in article 20 of the Covenant.

While mandated by article 20 of the Covenant, prohibitions against incitement must be crafted with care to comply with other provisions of the Covenant that protect freedom of opinion and freedom of expression. Freedom of expression is an essential foundation of democracy, and its enjoyment is linked with other important rights such as the freedom of thought, conscience and religion. Great care must be taken to ensure that any restriction on the right to freedom of expression is both necessary and proportional.

---

[49] The FATF Forty Recommendations on Money-Laundering, recommendation 2 *(b)*.

The Council of Europe Convention on the Prevention of Terrorism provides one model for analysing the above-mentioned questions. Its article 5, on public provocation to commit a terrorist offence, defines "provocation to commit a terrorist offence": "the distribution, or otherwise making available, of a message to the public, with the intent to incite the commission of a terrorist offence, where such conduct, whether or not directly advocating terrorist offences, causes a danger that one or more such offences may be committed".

That definition addresses four questions concerning the interaction of a provocation/incitement offence with freedom of expression:

(a)   Only public messages are criminalized, leaving non-public incitement to be dealt with under the general concepts of criminal responsibility, which may include complicity, criminal association, conspiracy, aiding and abetting, counselling, preparing, organizing, directing or contributing to offences;

(b)   Making a subjective intent (to incite the commission of a terrorist offence) an element of the offence eliminates many possible objections concerning freedom of expression and the value of intellectual discourse concerning unpopular ideas;

(c)   No legislative or executive authority is given power to declare that any particular message, slogan, symbol or philosophy is dangerous or prohibited per se. The offence element, that the message being publicized will cause the danger of the commission of a terrorist offence, must be proved to the satisfaction of an independent judiciary in a specific, factual context;

(d)   Proven conduct causing a danger of the commission of terrorist offences is punishable whether or not it involves direct advocacy of particular offences.

Exclusion of any justification

None of the criminalized terrorist acts can, under any circumstance, be justified by considerations of a political, philosophical, ideological, racial, ethnic, religious or other, similar nature. The corpus of international counter-terrorism instruments rests on an unequivocal condemnation of this type of crime, with no concession to any possibility of ideological justification.

Ultimately, no terrorist offence can be justified by considerations of a political nature. Including such exceptions in national legislation would serve to largely nullify the effect of the criminalizing provisions.

C.   Procedural law

Criminal procedural law constitutes one of the main safeguards of the rule of law and offers concrete legal safeguards to the rights of all those who come in contact with the criminal justice system. It plays the dual role of social protection through the prosecution process and protection of the accused by permitting the accused to defend himself or herself. It ensures the reliability of the criminal justice process and, in particular, the criminal trial, thus ensuring a fair justice system.

Effective action against terrorism may sometimes require specific amendments to procedural law. Such changes are often called for by the universal instruments against terrorism or are required in order to comply with various other State obligations under international law. A workable criminal justice response to terrorism almost certainly requires a review of existing procedural law, including its evidentiary requirements, in order to empower the criminal justice system to fulfil its security and social protection duties while upholding its commitment to the rule of law and human rights.

The determination of Member States to take strong action against terrorism has raised a number of issues in relation to the need to strengthen procedural safeguards to protect individual rights. In deploying their counter-terrorism strategies, States must continue to adhere to the rule of law, including the basic principles, standards and obligations under criminal and constitutional law that define the boundaries of permissible and legitimate criminal justice activities against terrorism. Those boundaries tend to be articulated to a large extent in various aspects of criminal procedural law and laws regulating police powers. Careful attention must therefore be paid when special counter-terrorism laws representing a departure from criminal law traditions are adopted.

The case law of international courts and tribunals, as well as domestic courts, show that some counter-terrorism measures have resulted in prolonged detention without charge, denial of the right to challenge the lawfulness of detention, denial of access to legal representation, illegal deportations, monitoring of conversation with lawyer, and incommunicado detention.[50]

It is necessary to be cautious when modifying normally applicable procedures in order to adapt them to the unique characteristics of terrorist crimes. Any substantial modification of criminal procedure is likely to raise fundamental questions about the protection of individual rights, the safeguarding of the rule of law and the integrity and the fairness of the criminal justice process. When national laws adopt special procedures to fight terrorism, particularly procedures that may potentially infringe on fundamental rights and freedoms, it is important to design safeguards to prevent any potential abuses.

Procedural and evidentiary mechanisms

A preventive strategy demands that lawful investigative and evidentiary mechanisms facilitate prosecutorial intervention before terrorist tragedies occur, while respecting the procedural protections embedded in the rule of law. For example, it would be an exercise in frustration to criminalize planning and preparation for terrorist attacks, and then not to permit the covert investigative techniques necessary to produce evidence of such plans and preparations.

Police powers

Police functions, powers and procedures are normally defined and limited by statute. Relevant legislation may include a police act, a code of criminal procedure and a criminal code. A police act typically encompasses organizational elements as well as the relevant powers of a police force, particularly in the public order realm. The police powers relating to investigation are likely to be found in the domestic criminal procedure code. In many instances in recent years, some of these powers have been enhanced by special legislation, often legislation adopted as a result of a terrorist incident or threat.

---

[50]*Countering Terrorism, Protecting Human Rights: a Manual*, p. 21.

Some experts argue that many of the investigative powers that Governments could use to penetrate terrorist organizations and defeat their plans—surveillance, informants, searches, seizures, wiretaps, arrests, interrogations, detentions—are too tightly restricted by a web of laws, judicial precedents and administrative rules. They argue that new legis-lation is necessary to make police powers more flexible and useful while simultaneously setting boundaries to minimize overuse or abuse.[51] (Some of these questions are addressed in Chapter III, on the role of law enforcement.)

Procedures relating to freezing, seizure and confiscation of assets

Actions to effectively prevent the financing of terrorist activities require not only the criminalization of certain conduct, but also implementation of procedures relating to the freezing, seizing and confiscation provisions as required by the treaty obligations of the International Convention for the Suppression of the Financing of Terrorism.[52] Article 8 of the Convention requires the following of States parties:

"*(a)* Each State party shall take appropriate measures, in accordance with its domestic legal principles, for the identification, detection and freezing or seizure of any funds used or allocated for the purpose of committing the offences set forth in article 2 as well as the proceeds derived from such offences, for purposes of possible forfeiture;

"*(b)* Each State party shall take appropriate measures, in accordance with its domestic legal principles, for the forfeiture of funds used or allocated for the purpose of committing the offences set forth in article 2 and the proceeds derived from such offences."

Unlike the broader freezing obligations under the freezing regimes imposed by the Security Council (see discussion below), the freezing, seizing and confiscation provisions of the International Convention for the Suppression of the Financing of Terrorism adopt the more traditional approach to the confiscation of criminal assets, based on the instrumentality and proceeds of crime principles.

Because terrorist violence is typically committed for ideological purposes rather than for profit, the Convention is not primarily a reactive tool to forfeit the proceeds of successful offences. The Convention focuses on reducing the incidence of terrorist acts by freezing, seizing and confiscating economic instrumentalities before they are used to support the commission of violent acts. This preventive purpose is emphasized in article 2, paragraph 3, of the Convention: "For an act to constitute an offence set forth in paragraph 1, it shall not be necessary that the funds were actually used to carry out an offence referred to in paragraph 1, subparagraphs *(a)* or *(b)*".

Some terrorist groups and incidents have been financed by various forms of common criminality. For example, the Madrid train bombings of 11 March 2004 were financed by property offences and drug dealing. However, the interdiction of terrorist financing, unlike money-laundering, would not be effective if limited to funds of illegal origin. To achieve its preventive purpose, the Convention requires that the provisional measures of freezing and seizing and the penalty of confiscation apply to any funds, whether their origin is lawful or unlawful, if those funds are provided or collected for use in terrorist acts.

---

[51]S. Taylor, "Rights, Liberty and Security: Recalibrating the Balance after September 11", in Martin G. (ed.), *The New Era of Terrorism: Selected Readings* (Sage Publications, 2004), p. 220.

[52]For examples of model legislation, see International Monetary Fund, *Suppressing the Financing of Terrorism: a Handbook for Legislative Drafting* (Washington, D.C., International Monetary Fund, 2003).

Freezing obligations also arise from two principal relevant resolutions of the Security Council: resolutions 1267 (1999) and 1373 (2001). Those resolutions impose wider-reaching freezing obligations based on membership of a particular group or the reasonable belief that a person or group has committed or attempted to commit a terrorist act. In its resolution 1267 (1999), the Security Council demanded that the Taliban cease certain actions supporting terrorism and turn over Osama bin Laden to a country where he would be brought to justice. In order to enforce that demand, it decided that all States shall freeze funds and other financial resources, including funds derived or generated from property owned or controlled directly or indirectly by the Taliban, or by any undertaking owned or controlled by the Taliban, as designated by the Committee established pursuant to that resolution.

Non-compliance with resolution 1267 (1999) by the Taliban led the Security Council, in December 2000, to expand, through its resolution 1333 (2000), the freezing obligations to cover also assets belonging to individuals and entities associated with Osama bin Laden and Al-Qaida. The sanctions regime was further refined by the Security Council in its resolution 1390 (2002), in which the Security Council decided that States shall take the following measures with respect to Osama bin Laden, members of the Al-Qaida organization and the Taliban and other individuals, groups, undertakings and entities associated with them:

Freeze without delay the funds and other financial assets or economic resources of these individuals, groups, undertakings and entities, including funds derived from property owned or controlled, directly or indirectly, by them or by persons acting on their behalf or at their direction, and ensure that neither these nor any other funds, financial assets or economic resources are made available, directly or indirectly, for such persons' benefit, by their nationals or by any persons within their territory.

In its resolution 1267 (1999) the Security Council also decided to establish the Al-Qaida and Taliban Sanctions Committee, consisting of all the Council members, which maintains a list of targeted individuals and entities, known as the "Consolidated List" because it consolidates alphabetically organized lists of Taliban-associated individuals, Taliban-associated entities, Al-Qaida-associated individuals and Al-Qaida-associated entities.[53] The Committee also maintains a list of individuals and entities removed from the Consolidated List.[54]

The potential indefinite freezing of lawfully acquired property, based upon a determination by a political body, continues to be the subject of controversy.[55] Several listed individuals have brought judicial challenges based upon international and regional human rights law, constitutional provisions and domestic procedural law. A summary of relevant litigation is found in the periodic reports of the Analytical Support and Sanctions Monitoring Team of the Al-Qaida and Taliban Sanctions Committee.[56]

[53]The Consolidated List is available at www.un.org/sc/committees/1267/consolist.shtml.

[54]A list of individuals and entities removed from the Consolidated List is available at www.un.org/sc/committees/1267/docs/Delisted.pdf.

[55]Watson Institute for International Studies of Brown University, "Strengthening Targeted Sanctions Through Fair and Clear Procedures", white paper prepared by the Watson Institute's Targeted Sanctions Project; the European Convention on Human Rights (2006), "Due Process and United Nations Security Council Counter-Terrorism Sanctions", report to the Council of Europe; B. Fassbinder, "Targeted Sanctions and Due Process", study commissioned by the Office of Legal Affairs of the Secretariat.

[56]Available at www.un.org/sc/committees/1267/monitoringteam.shtml.

In paragraph 1 *(c)* of its resolution 1373 (2001), the Council created freezing obligations aimed at funds and other financial assets or economic resources of persons who commit, or attempt to commit, terrorist acts; of entities owned or controlled directly or indirectly by such persons; and of persons and entities acting on behalf of, or at the direction of such persons and entities.

The resolution neither specifies particular individuals or entities whose funds must be frozen because they are involved with terrorist acts nor establishes a listing mechanism. It also does not define "terrorist act". The European Court of First Instance has commented on difficulties in applying paragraph 1 *(c)* of resolution 1373 (2001) owing to the absence of a universally accepted definition of the concepts of "terrorism" and "terrorist act" in international law.[57]

In the absence of a definitive explanation in Security Council resolution 1373 (2001) of what acts trigger its freezing obligation, countries apply their own interpretations. Many countries have definitions of terrorism or terrorist acts in domestic criminal statutes. Confiscation may then be possible as a criminal penalty under national law, but would be unlikely to reach all property required to be frozen pursuant to resolution 1373 (2001). That is because the resolution requires freezing all property of those who commit or support acts of terrorism, including property not intended for criminal use. Such property would not be subject to confiscation under code provisions that typically provide for the restraint and confiscation of only actual or intended instrumentalities and proceeds of crime. Implementation of the obligation imposed by resolution 1373 (2001) thus requires the creation of a freezing power in a court or other competent authority that exists independently of the criminal process.

Some countries and regional organizations create their own lists of foreign and domestic persons and entities that commit, attempt to commit or support terrorist acts and whose funds must be frozen. The Council of the European Union adopted common positions 1999/727/CFSP and 2001/931/CFSP and subsequent common positions and implemented regulations to give effect to Security Council resolutions 1267 (1999) and 1373 (2001) and their respective successor resolutions.

For countries seeking a template for the drafting of legislation on asset restraint and related issues, such as confiscation, the United Nations Office on Drugs and Crime and the International Monetary Fund have developed model legislation on money-laundering and financing of terrorism.[58]

Procedural Measures for the Protection of Witnesses and Informants

Witnesses and informants play an essential role in the investigation and prosecution of terrorist activities. Protecting them is often crucial to the success of the criminal justice process. A number of procedural measures can be considered in order to better protect witnesses and informants whose assistance is essential to the prevention, investigation and prosecution of terrorist crimes. These measures must ensure an appropriate balance between the need to protect the safety of witnesses and the obligation to safeguard the defendants' right to a fair trial.

---

[57]See the decision of the European Court of First Instance in *Organisation des Modjahedines du peuple d'Iran v. Council* (T-228/02).

[58]The model legislation is available at www.imf.org/external/np/leg/amlcft/eng/pdf/amlml05.pdf.

"The ability of a witness to give testimony in a judicial setting or to cooperate with law enforcement investigations without fear of intimidation or reprisal is essential to maintaining the rule of law."

Good Practices for the Protection of Witnesses in
Criminal Proceedings Involving Organized Crime, UNODC, p. 1.

- *Evidentiary rules:* To protect witnesses, States may consider procedural reforms of the kind envisaged in article 24 of the Organized Crime Convention, including providing evidentiary rules to permit witness testimony to be given in a manner that ensures the safety of the witness, such as permitting testimony to be given through the use of communications technology such as video links or other adequate means.

- *Recognition of pretrial statements:* In order to protect witnesses and informants, it is sometimes necessary to consider procedural means of recognizing pretrial statements. In most European countries, pretrial statements given by witnesses and collaborators of justice are recognized as valid evidence in court, provided that the parties have the opportunity to participate in the examination of witnesses.[59] A report by a Council of Europe group of experts suggests that one may assume that, in a system where pretrial statements of witnesses or testimonies of anonymous witnesses are generally regarded as valid evidence during proceedings, such procedures can provide effective protection of witnesses.[60]

- *The disclosure process:* Another promising procedural approach to the protection of witnesses and informants consists of facilitating the management of the disclosure process and mitigating the risk to which it can expose witnesses and potential witnesses.[61] In many justice systems, defence counsels have a right to obtain witness statements at the time of disclosure, but there is always a risk that this process may compromise the security of the witnesses or informants.

Anonymity of witnesses and informants

In many European countries, under exceptional circumstances and in accordance with European human rights law, persons who provide evidence in criminal proceedings may be granted anonymity in order to prevent their identification. In many civil law countries, the decision to grant the status of anonymous witness rests with the "judge of instruction", who must ascertain the risk to the witness as well as the identity, credibility and reliability of the witness.[62] This is done through an interview from which the accused, his/her attorney and the public prosecutor can be excluded. If excluded, those persons may follow the interview through an audio link with a voice transformer (or other secure means), and the defence must have an opportunity to ask questions (whether through the audio link or by submitting questions to the investigation judge before the interview).[63]

---

[59]N. Piancete, "Analytical Report", in Council of Europe, *Terrorism: Protection of Witnesses and Collaborators of Justice* (Strasbourg, France, Council of Europe, 2006), p. 22.

[60]Council of Europe, *Combating Organised Crime: Best Practice Surveys of the Council of Europe* (Strasbourg, France, Council of Europe, 2004), p. 22.

[61]For instance, the International Criminal Tribunal for the Former Yugoslavia considers delaying the disclosure of witness identity prior to trial as a measure that can be taken by the court to achieve the appropriate level of protection for a particular witness.

[62]For an examination of the rich body of case law yielding important principles of international human rights law on witness anonymity, see D. Lusty, "Anonymous Accusers: an Historical and Comparative Analysis of Secret Witnesses in Criminal Trials", *The Sydney Law Review*, 24, 2002, p. 363.

[63]Council of Europe, *Combating Organised Crime: Best Practice Surveys of the Council of Europe*, p. 19.

It is also often possible to grant partial anonymity to witnesses at risk. The defendant is given an opportunity to question the witnesses directly, but the witnesses do not have to state their names and addresses. In such cases, only the trial judge is informed of their identity. Some disguise preventing the accused from recognizing the witness, a measure used primarily to protect the identity of undercover police officers, is sometimes used to protect witnesses.

The European Court of Human Rights has often accepted the legality of the use of anonymous informants during preliminary investigations, but it has also emphasized that the use at the trial of the information thus obtained presents a problem with respect to fairness.[64] Even when permitted by law, the procedure for granting partial or full anonymity to a witness tends to be rarely used because, in practice, it can limit the admissibility of various elements of the testimony.[65] In some cases, if the examination of a witness in the presence of a defendant poses imminent danger to the health and safety of the witness, the witness can be heard in the absence of the defendant in order to prevent both direct verbal or physical threats to the witness as well as more subtle intimidation by the defendant, such as threatening looks or gestures.[66]

Anonymous testimonies raise certain issues about the rights of the defendants to a fair trial. The European Court of Human Rights has set some limits on the use of anonymous testimony.[67] The judge must know the identity of the witness and have heard the witness's testimony under oath and determined that it is credible and must have considered the reasons for the request of anonymity; the interests of the defence must be weighed against those of the witnesses, and the defendants and their counsel must have an opportunity to ask the witness questions; a condemnation cannot be based on the strength of the testimony of that witness alone.[68] According to the European Court of Human Rights, the admissibility of such anonymous testimony depends on the circumstances of the case and three principles that emerge from case law:[69] Is anonymity justified by compelling reasons? Have the resulting limitations on the effective exercise of the rights of the defence been adequately compensated for? Was the conviction exclusively or substantially based on such an anonymous testimony? Special rules on anonymity have been legislated in Belgium, Finland, France, Germany, the Netherlands, and the Republic of Moldova.[70] Under the legislation of some States (e.g. Republic of Moldova), the testimony of an anonymous witness must be corroborated in order for it to be considered valid.

---

[64]Ibid., p. 31.

[65]Ibid., p. 20.

[66]Ibid., p. 20.

[67]European Court of Human Rights, *Visser v. the Netherlands*, 14 February 2002.

[68]X. Lameyre and M. Cardoso, "La délation en droit pénal français, une pratique qui ne dit pas son nom", in J. P. Brodeur and F. Jobard (eds.), *Citoyens et délateurs—La délation peut-elle être civique ?* (Paris, Éditions Autrement, 2005), p. 152.

[69]Council of Europe, *Terrorism: Special Investigation Techniques* (Strasbourg, France, Council of Europe, 2005), p. 31; The European Court of Human Rights, through its judgements, has played an important role by "establishing legal limits within which the battle against organized crime in Europe must be waged", in particular with respect to the use of undercover agents and anonymous witnesses: see C. Fignaut and L. Paoli (eds.), *Organized Crime in Europe—Concepts, Patterns and Control Policies in the European Union and Beyond* (Dordrecht, the Netherlands, Springer, 2004), p. 628.

[70]N. Piancete, "Analytical Report", p. 19.

The International Criminal Defence Attorneys Association, in its submission to the Preparatory Commission for the International Criminal Court on rules of procedure and evidence, stated that "complete witness anonymity is only appropriate in instances where the individual is an informant who aided in the discovery of admissible evidence, but is not testifying against the accused in the proceeding".[71]

Periodic review of legislation

The need to take decisive action to protect human security may lead a State to urgently adopt new counter-terrorism measures, sometimes without having had a chance to fully examine their implications from a human rights or rule-of-law perspective. Legislative reforms are sometimes adopted on an emergency basis. Hence, it is important to conduct periodic reviews of legislation, particularly when the pressing circumstances that led to the adoption of the legislation have subsided.

Judicial oversight is case-specific and dependant on the resources of litigants to engage in the process. Other mechanisms can be contemplated to subject special dispositions to scrutiny such as, for example, appointing a special reviewer (as in the United Kingdom of Great Britain and Northern Ireland), a congressional review (as in the United States of America), or a review by a parliamentary committee (as in Canada). Review by democratically elected politicians may further public accountability.

Some countries have placed a specific review requirement in their counter-terrorism legislation, or even a sunset clause. Such a mandated review permits the scrutiny of the law from a rule-of-law perspective. The purpose of the review is to establish whether the objectives of the law (security) are furthered in a manner consistent with the rule of law and respect for human rights. Such a review can be useful when there are concerns about the swiftness with which the legislation has been adopted or about the nature of the new provisions or when there are uncertainties about the implementation and application of the measures introduced by the legislation.

[71]International Criminal Defence Attorneys Association, "Protection of Witnesses", position paper submitted to the Preparatory Commission for the International Criminal Court on rules of procedure and evidence, 26 July-13 August 1999, p. 2.

III. Role of law enforcement

The police and other law enforcement officials face particular challenges in responding to terrorism within a rule-of-law and human rights framework. Capacity limitations often emerge when the police face a terrorist conspiracy, particularly one that is inter-national in nature. Given the difficulties involved in detecting, investigating and controlling terrorist activities, let alone preventing terrorist violence, police agencies must consider ways of enhancing their technical, human and strategic capacity to respond to terrorism. Given the international dimension of many terrorist activities, police services must also develop their capacity for law enforcement cooperation. Finally, because of the complexity and the sensitivity of counter-terrorist operations, it is important for all law enforcement agencies to establish sound mechanisms for governance and leadership, accountability and the protection of integrity.

Duty of police

"In the performance of their duty, law enforcement officials shall respect and protect human dignity and maintain and uphold the human rights of all persons."

Code of Conduct for Law Enforcement Officials
(General Assembly resolution 34/169, annex)

In countering terrorism, the police are required to work closely with the military and intelligence services. There is a risk that this may blur the distinction between the police and the army, contribute to the militarization of the police, and weaken civilian control and oversight of the police. Unless the integrity and independence of police are protected, the fight against terrorism may lead to the politicization of the police, which could undermine its legitimacy and credibility in the eyes of the population. For that reason, States must clearly define and circumscribe the function of the police in counter-terrorism measures.

The police need to carry out their function in a non-arbitrary and impartial manner, without political interference. While that requires a degree of operational independence, safeguards are important because too much autonomy may lead to abuses of authority. To maintain that delicate balance, the police need to operate in an environment of transparency and must be held accountable for their actions.

This chapter considers a number of crucial issues, including the use of effective and legitimate investigation methods, the use of the powers of arrest and detention, the use of effective and legitimate interrogation techniques and the prevention of various forms of obstruction of justice. Special attention will be given to witness protection, the investigation of money-laundering and financing of terrorism offences and international law enforcement cooperation.

A. Methods of investigation

The clandestine nature of terrorist conspiracies and activities and the typical mode of operation of terrorist organizations require specialized investigation methods. Several international and regional human rights bodies have highlighted the risk of discrimination presented by some law enforcement methods used to counter terrorism. Generally speaking, the use of police investigation methods that may compromise the rights of individuals can be justified only on reasonable grounds based on the principles of necessity and proportionality. In determining whether the police are justified, in special circumstances, in departing from normal and approved police practices, one can use the following criteria and interpret them as restrictively as possible:

Necessity: Is the measure really necessary and are there not other, less invasive or harmful measures that could be used to achieve the same aim?

Effectiveness: Has it been proven or is there a reasonable, objective basis to believe that the measure can achieve the ends for which it has been conceived?

Harm: To what extent is the measure affecting the rights of individuals?

Secondary effect: Is the measure likely to produce any undesirable secondary effects, including possibly affecting the overall capacity of the police to work effectively with a particular community or the willingness of the community to cooperate with the police? Is the measure likely to contribute to the stigmatization of certain groups?

Offender profiling and group targeting

In conducting counter-terrorism investigations, it is often difficult to identify potential suspects. Because certain communities can be associated with terrorist activities, the police may be tempted to focus on those particular communities in order to prevent terrorist incidents from taking place. However, racial profiling or profiling on the basis of religion is not a legitimate response to those challenges. The Committee on the Elimination of Racial Discrimination has called on States to "ensure that any measures taken in the fight against terrorism do not discriminate, in purpose or effect, on the grounds of race, colour, descent or national or ethnic origin and that non-citizens are not subjected to racial or ethnic profiling or stereotyping."[72]

"No difference in treatment which is based exclusively or to a decisive extent on a person's ethnic origin is capable of being justified in a contemporary democratic society built on the principles of pluralism and respect for different cultures."

European Court of Human Rights, 13 December 2005, *Timishev v. Russia*, para. 42.

While profiles based on factors that are statistically proven to correlate with certain criminal conduct may be effective tools when law enforcement resources are limited, the use of broad profiles that reflect unexamined generalizations or stereotypes is extremely problematic. Profiling based on stereotypical assumptions that persons of a certain "race", national or ethnic origin or religion are particularly likely to commit crime may lead to practices that are incompatible with the principle of non-discrimination. The Special Rapporteur has expressed his grave concern that law enforcement authorities in various

[72]General recommendation XXX on discrimination against non-citizens, adopted by the Committee on the Elimination of Racial Discrimination at its sixty-fifth session (*Official Records of the General Assembly, Fifty-ninth Session, Supplement No. 18* (A/59/18), chap. VIII, para. 10).

States have adopted counter-terrorism practices that are based on terrorist profiles that include characteristics such as a person's presumed race, ethnicity, national origin or religion.

The Special Rapporteur on the promotion and protection of human rights and fundamental freedoms while countering terrorism has also noted that terrorist profiles based on national or ethnic origin and religion are also being used, for example, in the context of immigration controls. The practice of terrorist profiling raises concerns with respect to a number of human rights. Data mining initiatives based on broad terrorist profiles that include group characteristics such as religion and national origin may constitute a disproportionate and thus arbitrary interference with the right to privacy, which is guaranteed by article 17 of the International Covenant on Civil and Political Rights. The Special Rapporteur expressed a concern that profiling based on stereotypical assumptions may bolster sentiments of hostility and xenophobia in the general public towards persons of certain ethnic or religious backgrounds.

States must strengthen border controls as one way of identifying security threats at the point of entry. However, in the view of the United Nations High Commissioner for Refugees, profiling and screening solely on the basis of religious or racial characteristics is discriminatory and inappropriate.[34] Early identification of terrorist suspects can be facilitated through various security checks and through enhanced cooperation between border guards, intelligence services and immigration and asylum authorities of the States concerned, as well as with organizations such as the International Criminal Police Organization (INTERPOL) and the European Police Office (Europol).

To prevent racial and other unjustifiable profiling practices, it may be necessary for a State to adopt legislation to specifically prohibit it. National legislation prohibiting racial discrimination should specifically cover the activity of the police. It may also be useful for a State to review its legislation to determine whether it sufficiently defines "reasonable suspicion standards" with respect to various police investigation and intervention practices. If the law does not already provide a "reasonable suspicion standard", it may be necessary to introduce one whereby powers relating to control, surveillance and investigation activities can be exercised only on the basis of a suspicion that is founded on objective criteria.

It may be necessary, when there are credible reports of unacceptable profiling and targeting practices, to conduct an audit of police practices to review policies, training curricula, supervisory methods and operational protocols. When administrative mechanisms to carry out such an audit do not exist, it may be necessary to establish an independent authority to carry out such a review. A review of police statistics and data broken down by language, religion or nationality may provide an initial assessment of potential discriminatory practices.

Police practices can be improved by providing training on racial profiling and existing standards establishing a "reasonable suspicion". It is also essential to ensure effective investigations by an independent body or a civilian oversight mechanism of alleged cases of racial discrimination or racially motivated misconduct by the police, and to ensure that the perpetrators of those acts are adequately punished. Finally, measures must be taken to make it possible and safe for victims of racial and other forms of unacceptable profiling and discrimination to report those incidents to the authorities.[73]

---

[73]Specific recommendations are offered by the European Commission against Racism and Intolerance in its ECRI General Policy Recommendation No. 11 on combating racism and racial discrimination in policing, adopted on 29 June 2007.

Gathering intelligence

The acquisition, analysis and use of information about terrorist groups are essential to prevent acts of terrorism. Information may be collected through open and covert sources and may be obtained from other police agencies at home or abroad. Information-gathering can be improved through technology but also by cultivating relationships with other stake-holders, such as the community, other law enforcement agencies, intelligence agencies and foreign Governments.

Intelligence-gathering activities, in particular covert surveillance, must be regulated by law, monitored by independent agencies and subject to judicial review. Any act that impacts on a person's privacy must be prescribed and regulated by law. Thus, any search, surveillance or data collection related to an individual must be authorized by law. Laws authorizing interference with personal privacy must specify in detail the precise circumstances in which the interference is to be permitted and must not be implemented in a discriminatory manner.

Article 17 of the International Covenant on Civil and Political Rights prohibits States parties from interfering with the privacy of those within the State's jurisdiction, and it requires States to protect those persons by law against arbitrary or unlawful interference with their privacy. Recent counter-terrorism strategies have included efforts to collect, analyse and use information about large numbers of individuals. Many States have significantly expanded the surveillance powers and capacity of their law enforcement agencies (including wiretapping, use of tracking devices and monitoring of Internet communications). Those authorized law enforcement practices have the potential to limit the privacy of the individuals concerned. Their use also raises questions about how the data collected are to be protected, stored and, when necessary, shared with other agencies.

When personal information is collected, it must be protected against unlawful or arbitrary access, disclosure or use. There should be provisions for individuals to ascertain whether their personal data are stored for law enforcement purposes and to be able to rectify or remove incorrect data.

Intelligence systems and the sharing of information

The nature of terrorist threats necessitates the gathering and analysis of information that is not confined by territorial borders or organizational structure.[74] The sharing of information and intelligence between security and law enforcement agencies is an important means of preventing terrorist acts and other major criminal offences. Efforts to increase such exchanges have produced some positive results but have also shown that, in many instances, the domestic and international legal frameworks governing such exchanges are inadequate.

Some progress is being made at the bilateral, subregional and regional levels to ensure that current exchange mechanisms meet the needs of judicial and law enforcement cooperation, while providing the necessary safeguards for the protection of personal data and individual privacy rights. The Treaty of Prüm, of 27 May 2005, whose original signatories were Austria, Belgium, France, Germany, Luxembourg, the Netherlands and

---

[74]Eveline R. Hertzberger, *Counter-Terrorism Intelligence Cooperation in the European Union* (Turin, UNICRI, 2007), p. 27.

Spain and which has been included in the legal framework of the European Union, is an example of an initiative designed to help States improve the sharing of information for preventing and combating terrorist crimes, cross-border crime and illegal immigration.[75] Reference is also to be made to the 2006 Council of the European Union framework decision on simplifying the exchange of information and intelligence between law enforcement authorities of the Member States of the European Union,[76] which lays out the basic principles for the effective and expeditious exchange of information and intelligence for the purpose of conducting criminal investigations or criminal intelligence operations. Each State has a responsibility to provide the legal and regulatory frameworks that will guide these exchanges across systems and to ensure that they do not compromise the integrity of the criminal justice process or the criminal justice agencies involved.

Use of criminal informants and accomplices

When attempting to break up criminal and terrorist conspiracies and prevent terrorist crimes, the police often need to rely on the testimonies of co-defendants and accomplices willing to cooperate and provide evidence against their former associates.[77] Although some may argue that there is insufficient evidence about the effectiveness of that particular approach,[78] the use of criminal informants and accomplices is usually considered essential to the successful detection and prosecution of terrorism and organized crime.[79] As a result, various international agreements and conventions actively promote these methods.[80] National laws are sometimes also necessary to authorize these practices and to determine how and when evidence obtained through such sources can be used against the accused.

Because of the importance of "accomplice testimony" in cases involving terrorism, plea bargaining and offers of immunity or leniency often play a crucial role in the gathering of evidence and the successful prosecution of these cases. Therefore, in practice, witness protection measures, as a means of eliciting cooperation from criminal informants, are intertwined with other measures such as plea bargaining, immunity from prosecution and reduced sentences.

Formal agreements are often struck between the informant and the police clarifying the obligations of both parties. In most countries, however, there remains a need to provide a tighter framework for the management of informants, in the form of guidelines, statutory regulations and increased independent oversight.

---

[75]Ibid., pp. 89-90.

[76]Council of the European Union framework decision 2006/960/JHA of 18 December 2006 on simplifying the exchange of information and intelligence between law enforcement authorities of the member States of the European Union (*Official Journal of the European Union*, L 386, 29 December 2006).

[77]Council of Europe, *Combating Organised Crime: Best Practice Surveys of the Council of Europe*, p. 22; A. J. Schreiber, "Dealing with the Devil: an examination of the FBI's troubled relationship with its confidential informants", *Columbia Journal of Law and Social Problems*, vol. 34, No. 4 (2001), pp. 301-368.

[78]N. R. Fyfe and J. Sheptycki, *Facilitating Witness Co-operation in Organised Crime Cases: An International Review*, Home Office Online Report 27/0 (London, Home Office, 2005); also N. R. Fyfe and J. Sheptycki, "International trends in the facilitation of witness co-operation in organized crime cases", *European Journal of Criminology*, vol. 3, No. 3 (2006), pp. 319-355.

[79]For example, J. P. Laborde, *État de droit et crime organisé* (Paris, Dalloz, 2005).

[80]For example, the Organized Crime Convention and Council of Europe recommendation Rec(2001)11 of the Committee of Ministers to member States concerning guiding principles on the fight against organized crime, adopted by the Committee of Ministers on 19 September 2001.

Use of modern investigation techniques

The effectiveness of techniques such as electronic surveillance, undercover operations and controlled deliveries cannot be overemphasized. Those techniques are especially useful in dealing with sophisticated groups because of the inherent difficulties and dangers involved in gaining access to information and gathering intelligence on their operations. Technological advances such as cross-border surveillance using satellites and the interception of telephone conversations through satellite connections make cross-border investigation possible without the physical presence of a foreign investigating officer.

Domestic arrangements and legislation relating to these techniques must be reviewed to reflect technological developments, taking full account of any human rights implications and the need to facilitate international cooperation. Wherever special investigation techniques have the potential to interfere with guaranteed rights, they must be subject to effective control by bodies independent of the person or agency implementing them.

New technological developments and modern methods of investigation have created new issues with respect to the legitimacy of these methods and the protection of the rights of the individuals involved in the course of an investigation. The police, prosecutors and the courts have a duty to ensure that these methods are used lawfully and in accordance with applicable human rights standards.

Prosecutors must be very vigilant in their use of evidence obtained through such "modern" methods. The legal basis for cooperation in criminal matters for officers acting under cover or under an assumed identity is not always strong. For prosecutors and courts, there are questions about the admissibility of evidence collected in other States through methods that are not necessarily acceptable in their own State and about the use of evidence obtained by officials in another State in violation of the law of that State. The verification of the legitimacy of evidence obtained as a result of international police cooperation is certainly not without procedural and practical difficulties.

B. Arrest and detention

Depriving individuals of their personal liberty is one of the most common means of controlling and preventing crime and terrorism. The terms "arrest" and "detention" are often used interchangeably, but they refer to different concepts. According to the Body of Principles for the Protection of All Persons under Any Form of Detention or Imprisonment,[81] an "arrest" refers to the act of apprehending a person for the alleged commission of an offence or by the action of an authority. The arrest, therefore, may take place on criminal grounds and be reviewed by a judge, or may be administratively ordered ("by the action of an authority"). Arrested persons are often, but not necessarily, detained.

The lawful application of the powers to arrest and detain must be restricted by law to specific conditions that are described clearly in the law and for which subsequent accountability is required. The key human rights principles that must guide the lawful application of the powers to arrest and detain are the following:

- The arrest and the detention must be lawful and not arbitrary;
- The arrest and detention must be in accordance with procedures established by law;

---

[81] General Assembly resolution 43/173, annex.

- Individuals who have been arrested or are being detained must be treated in accordance with the principle of presumption of innocence and should be detained separately from convicted persons;

- Specific and precise time limits should be set by law for the prompt appearance of the arrested/detained person before a judicial authority;

- The arrested/detained person must have access to legal counsel and must be able to communicate with counsel in full confidentiality;

- The arrested/detained person must be informed of the reasons for the arrest/detention, the charges against him/her, in a language that he or she can understand;

- The arrested/detained person must be informed of his/her rights, including the right to legal counsel;

- The date, time and reason for the arrest, the identity of the person arrested or detained, the identity of the person(s) who performed the arrest and the time and date of the person's first appearance before a judicial authority must all be duly recorded;

- The arrested/detained person has the right to access to the outside world;

- The arrested/detained person has the right to take proceedings before a court, in order for the court to decide on the lawfulness of the arrest and/or the detention (habeas corpus).

The "reasonableness" of the suspicion on which an arrest must be based forms an essential part of the safeguard against arbitrary arrest and detention

"[H]aving a "reasonable suspicion" presupposes the existence of facts or information which would satisfy an objective observer that the person concerned may have committed the offence. What may be regarded as "reasonable" will, however, depend upon all the circumstances. In this respect, terrorist crime falls into a special category. Because of the attendant risk of loss of life and human suffering, the police are obliged to act with utmost urgency in following up all information, including information from secret sources. Further, the police may frequently have to arrest a suspected terrorist on the basis of information which is reliable but which cannot, without putting in jeopardy the source of the information, be revealed to the suspect or produced in court to support a charge."

European Court of Human Rights, *Fox, Campbell and Hartley v. the United Kingdom*, 30 August 1990, paragraphs 32 and 34.

Arrest on the basis of ethnic profiling contradicts the principle that an arrest should never be arbitrary. That rejection of arbitrariness implies that someone should not be arrested or stopped or searched, for discriminatory reasons.

Prohibition of arbitrary arrest and detention

Article 9, paragraph 3, of the International Covenant on Civil and Political Rights requires that, in criminal cases, any person arrested or detained has to be brought promptly before a judge or other officer authorized by law to exercise judicial power. The person who is being arrested is entitled to take proceedings before a court in order for that court to decide without delay on the lawfulness of the arrest/detention and to order the release of that person if the detention is unlawful.

"No law enforcement official may inflict, instigate or tolerate any act of torture or other cruel, inhuman or degrading treatment or punishment, nor may any law enforcement official invoke superior orders or exceptional circumstances such as a state of war or a threat of war, a threat to national security, internal political instability or any other public emergency as a justification of torture or other cruel, inhuman or degrading treatment or punishment."

Code of Conduct for Law Enforcement Officials
(General Assembly resolution 34/169, annex, article 5).

There is no precise or universally authoritative answer to the question of how many hours or days the rule of law permits a person to be detained before being charged or released. However, the Human Rights Committee of the Office of the United Nations High Commissioner for Human Rights (OHCHR), established to monitor compliance with the International Covenant on Civil and Political Rights, stated, in its general comment No. 8 of 1982, that more precise time limits were fixed by law in most States parties and, in the view of the Committee, delays must not exceed a few days.

Article 9 of the International Covenant on Civil and Political Rights

"1. Everyone has the right to liberty and security of person. No one shall be subjected to arbitrary arrest or detention. No one shall be deprived of his liberty except on such grounds and in accordance with such procedure as are established by law.

"2. Anyone who is arrested shall be informed, at the time of arrest, of the reasons for his arrest and shall be promptly informed of any charges against him.

"3. Anyone arrested or detained on a criminal charge shall be brought promptly before a judge or other officer authorized by law to exercise judicial power and shall be entitled to trial within a reasonable time or to release. It shall not be the general rule that persons awaiting trial shall be detained in custody, but release may be subject to guarantees to appear for trial, at any other stage of the judicial proceedings, and, should occasion arise, for execution of the judgement.

"4. Anyone who is deprived of his liberty by arrest or detention shall be entitled to take proceedings before a court, in order that court may decide without delay on the lawfulness of his detention and order his release if the detention is not lawful.

"5. Anyone who has been the victim of unlawful arrest or detention shall have an enforceable right to compensation."

Right to notification and communication at the time of arrest

A person who is arrested is entitled to be informed of his or her rights, to know what he/she is being accused of, and to consult with counsel immediately following arrest. In the case of a foreign national, the universal anti-terrorism conventions and protocols and the Vienna Convention on Consular Relations[82] all require that the person has the right to communicate with and be visited by a representative of the State of which he or she is a national. In the case of a stateless person, the person has the right to communicate with the International Committee of the Red Cross and be visited by a representative of the State in whose territory that person habitually resides and to be informed of his or her rights.

---

[82]United Nations, *Treaty Series*, vol. 596, No. 8638.

Concerning the right to assistance from a defence lawyer, the Human Rights Committee has expressed concern about counter-terrorism measures that deny detainees access to counsel immediately following arrest.[83] The need for a measure providing for a time limit—which must be short—for granting such access can be justified but must be in conformity with the requirements of articles 9 and 14 of the International Covenant.

Following an arrest, individuals are frequently detained in police detention facilities. In such cases, the police have an obligation to ensure the safety and health of those individuals.[84] The police must also ensure that the individual is not, while in its custody, subjected to torture or other cruel, inhuman or degrading treatment or punishment.

Many countries will find it necessary to carefully review their policies, operational procedures, policy directives and training programmes related to police practices regarding arrest and temporary detention of suspects.

C. Interrogation and interviewing of suspects

The interview of a suspect is an investigative method to collect information that can further the investigation or be used as evidence at the trial. The use of the method must be guided by the principle of the presumption of innocence. The right to remain silent is inherent in the presumption of innocence. Furthermore, article 14, paragraph 3 *(g)* of the International Covenant on Civil and Political Rights states that everyone is entitled "not to be compelled to testify against himself or to confess guilt". Principle 21 of the Body of Principles for the Protection of All Persons under Any Form of Detention or Imprisonment is also quite explicit:

> "1. It shall be prohibited to take undue advantage of the situation of a detained or imprisoned person for the purpose of compelling him to confess, to incriminate himself otherwise or to testify against any another person.
>
> "2. No detained person while being interrogated shall be subject to violence, threats or methods of interrogation which impair his capacity of decision or his judgement."

The Body of Principles, in its principle 23, also provide guidance concerning recording the conduct of the interrogation/interview: "The duration of any interrogation of a detained or imprisoned person and of the intervals between interrogations as well as the identity of the officials who conducted the interrogations and other persons present shall be recorded and certified in such form as may be prescribed by law."

There is an absolute prohibition of torture and other cruel, inhuman or degrading treatment. Article 7 of the International Covenant states that "no one shall be subjected to torture or to cruel, inhuman or degrading treatment or punishment." A comprehensive definition of "torture" is provided in the Convention against Torture and Other Cruel, Inhuman or Degrading Treatment or Punishment.

---

[83]Report of the Secretary-General on the protection of human rights and fundamental freedoms while countering terrorism (A/58/266).

[84]Code of Conduct for Law Enforcement Officials, article 6 (General Assembly resolution 34/169, annex).

Article 1 of the Convention against Torture

"For the purposes of this Convention, the term "torture" means any act by which severe pain or suffering, whether physical or mental, is intentionally inflicted on a person for such purposes as obtaining from him or a third person information or a confession, punishing him for an act he or a third person has committed or is suspected of having committed, or intimidating or coercing him or a third person, or for any reason based on discrimination of any kind, when such pain or suffering is inflicted by or at the instigation of or with the consent or acquiescence of a public official or other person acting in an official capacity. It does not include pain or suffering arising only from, inherent in or incidental to lawful sanctions."

Information obtained through torture or other forms of coercion should not be accepted as evidence in court. Principle 27 of the Body of Principles for the Protection of All Persons under Any Form of Detention or Imprisonment stipulates that "non-compliance with these principles in obtaining evidence shall be taken into account in determining the admissibility of such evidence against a detained or imprisoned person".

In recent years, the question of torture and ill-treatment has come up in many contexts with respect to counter-terrorism measures. On 22 November 2001, the Committee against Torture of OHCHR issued a statement to States parties to the Convention against Torture and Other Cruel, Inhuman or Degrading Treatment or Punishment to remind them of the "non-derogable nature of most of the obligations undertaken by them" in ratifying the Convention against Torture. The Committee has repeatedly expressed its concern that interrogation techniques incompatible with article 7 of the International Covenant on Civil and Political Rights are still allegedly used and the "necessity defence" argument, which is not recognized under the Covenant, is often invoked and retained as a justification for interrogation methods that amount to a form of torture.

"The requirements of the investigation and the undeniable difficulties inherent in the fight against crime, particularly with regard to terrorism, cannot result in limits being placed on the protection to be afforded in respect of the physical integrity of individuals."

European Court of Human Rights, *Tomasi v. France*, 27 August 1992, para. 115.

An issue of concern with respect to the interrogation of detained terrorist suspects is the fear that impermissible coercive measures will be used, even if they do not reach the level of "severe pain or suffering" prohibited by the Convention against Torture. Measures creating discomfort may be unavoidable for custodial purposes and to ensure the safety of the guarding or interrogating personnel. However, if the discomfort is not justified by legitimate custodial and safety needs and its purpose is to overbear the will of the person being interrogated to secure information, it is impermissible under article 14, paragraph 3 *(g)* of the International Covenant.

D.   Preventing obstructions of justice

Various forms of obstruction of justice can hinder the efforts of the justice system to investigate and prosecute terrorist offences. Obstruction can include witness tampering and intimidation,[85] jury tampering and intimidation of justice officials.[86] Measures must be in place to prevent all forms of obstruction of justice and to deal severely with all attempts to obstruct the criminal justice process.

The particular situation of vulnerable groups and communities within a society requires attention. These groups can become subject to community-wide intimidation by terrorist and criminal groups. It is therefore important to address this kind of intimidation in order to prevent terrorism. Broader strategies are often required to protect whole communities against intimidation and retaliation by terrorist organizations and their sympathizers. The issue of community intimidation,[87] which is often related to various forms of discrimination, must be approached from a broad perspective. The communities that are targeted, intimidated and exploited by terrorist groups must feel safe enough to co-operate with the authorities. Members of such communities must believe that they will not be left on their own should they muster the courage to inform the authorities. Above all, it is important to ensure that counter-terrorism practices do not render these communities even more vulnerable to intimidation and coercion by radical or terrorist groups.

Community-wide intimidation involves "acts that are intended to create a general sense of fear and an attitude of non-cooperation with police and prosecutors within a particular community".[88] This can become particularly important for some communities when terrorist supporters attempt to compromise potential witnesses and expose them to potential prosecution for associating with terrorist elements.[89] Fear of reprisal and fear of ostracism play a role. Community-wide intimidation is especially frustrating for the police and prosecutors because, while no actionable threat is ever made in a given case, witnesses and victims are still effectively discouraged from testifying.[90]

Experts distinguish between "low-level" intimidation and the very serious and often life-threatening experience of other witnesses and their families, often in relation to organized criminal or terrorist groups. The number of witnesses who are exposed to the most serious threats is relatively small in comparison to the number of witnesses who face low-level intimidation, but it is the former group that tends to receive the most attention from law enforcement and justice officials. Both forms are encountered in the way in which terrorist and criminal groups typically maintain entire groups or communities in fear of reprisals and retaliation.

---

[85]S. Roadcap, "Obstruction of justice", *American Criminal Law Review*, vol. 41, vol. 2 (2004), pp. 911-945.

[86]J. P. Laborde, *État de droit et crime organisé* ..., p. 33.

[87]For example, K. M. Healey, "Victim and witness intimidation: new developments and emerging responses", *NIJ Research in Action* (Washington, D.C., National Institute of Justice, October 1995); N. R. Fyfe and H. McKay, "Desperately seeking safety", *British Journal of Criminology*, vol. 40, No. 4 (2000), pp. 675-691; N. R. Fyfe, *Protecting Intimidated Witnesses* (Hampshire, Ashgate, 2001), p. 18.

[88]K. Dedel, *Witness Intimidation*, Problem-Oriented Guides for Police, Problem-Specific Guides Series, No. 42 (Washington, D.C., United States Department of Justice, Office of Community Oriented Policing Services, 2006), p. 4.

[89]Y. Dandurand and V. Chin, "Human security objectives and the fight against transnational organized crime", *The Current Stage in Transnational Organized Crime: World and Japan*, Kan Ueda, ed., Human Security and Transnational Organized Crime Series (Kyoto, Nihon Hyouronsya, 2007), vol. 2, pp. 149-171.

[90]P. Finn and K. M. Healey, *Preventing Gang- and Drug-related Witness Intimidation*, National Institute of Justice Issues and Practices (Washington, D.C., United States Department of Justice, Office of Justice Programs, 1996), p. 4.

To further complicate matters, indirect witness intimidation can also occur in at least two ways:

- It can be committed by a third party—someone who was not directly involved in the crime being investigated or prosecuted;

- It can target someone close to the witnesses instead of the witnesses themselves (e.g. intimidating the spouse of a witness or other family members), sometimes even when those individuals live in a different country.

Intimidation of witnesses or justice officials can be overt or implicit (implicit intimidation involves a real but unexpressed threat of harm). The risk of collaborating with the justice system is heightened by the power wielded by those involved in terrorist activities, their ability to intimidate or suppress the witnesses and informants and the relative inability of the justice system to offer full protection to those witnesses.[91]

The various types of obstruction of justice must be clearly defined and criminalized in law and include provisions for severe punishment. The police have a duty to investigate and help prosecute all forms of obstructions of justice. These offences must be taken seriously, as they jeopardize the integrity of criminal justice process as a whole.

E. Witness protection measures and programmes

In contrast to the situation of victims of other types of serious crimes, victims of terrorism may have little if any relevant evidence to provide, and other physical or material evidence in such cases is often very limited. In that context, the testimonies of some witnesses, by virtue of their personal proximity to the planning or commission of the crime, can greatly assist the authorities in investigation or prosecution.[92] The protection of such individuals therefore takes on a great significance, even as it raises a number of practical, ethical and legal issues. The capacity of police agencies to offer effective protection must therefore be developed in two areas: the capacity to offer basic protection to witnesses and the availability of a formal witness relocation and protection programme.

Basic witness protection measures

The sheer complexity of witness intimidation means that a range of measures is required to tackle the problem.[93] The risk of intimidation can be reduced by minimizing the risk of witnesses being identified when they report a crime or a conspiracy or offer a statement and by protecting their anonymity and privacy. Protection programmes and measures are often in place for witnesses who are exposed to serious danger, but far less attention is given to addressing low-level threats or community-wide forms of intimidation.[94]

A second tier of protection includes practical measures such as offering witnesses the use of alarms, calling devices and other crime prevention devices; offering quick access to police assistance and other services; conducting a security audit of an individual's home;

---

[91]Anne-Marie Boisvert, *La protection des collaborateurs de la justice: éléments de mise à jour de la politique québécoise; rapport final présenté au ministre de la Sécurité publique* (Quebec, 2005), p. 8.

[92]Council of Europe, *Combating Organised Crime* ..., p. 20.

[93]N. R. Fyfe, *Protecting Intimidated Witnesses* ..., p. 47.

[94]Australia, Victoria, Office of Policy Integrity, *Review of the Victoria Police Witness Protection Program; report of the Director, Police Integrity* (Melbourne, Victorian Government Printer, 2005), p. 8.

giving witnesses the option of visiting the police station instead of being interviewed where they live or work and other means of reducing the likelihood of contact between them and offenders; transporting them to and from work, school or the court; keeping witnesses separate from offenders whenever they must be at the police station or in the courthouse; offering them emergency or short-term relocation as required; or seeking "no-contact" court orders on their behalf.[95] In any given case, a combination of several of these measures is usually required. As the witness's situation evolves, the risk may change and must be reassessed, and a different set of measures may become necessary.

The effective protection of witnesses and collaborators of justice requires a police capacity to assess the risk faced by those individuals and to respond quickly to direct threats.

Witness protection programmes

Witness protection programmes can also offer a way to safeguard the investigation and the criminal trial and ensure the security of the witnesses. Their main objective is to safeguard the lives and personal security of witnesses and collaborators of justice and people close to them. The programmes include procedures for the physical protection of witnesses and collaborators of justice such as, to the extent necessary and feasible, relocating them, providing them with new identity documents and permitting, where appropriate, non-disclosure or limitations on the disclosure of information concerning the new identity and whereabouts of such persons. Even if it is not uncommon for a witness to be rewarded for cooperation with law enforcement authorities (financially, by charge reduction as a result of plea bargaining or by leniency at the time of sentencing), witness protection programmes are not some kind of reward for the witness for cooperating with the authorities.[96]

A working group composed of the International Institute of Higher Studies in Criminal Sciences (ISISC), the Monitoring Centre on Organized Crime (OPCO) and Europol recommended that specialized witness protection units be established with adequate administrative, operational, budgetary and informational technology autonomy.[97] The group of experts emphasized that such units should not be involved in the investigation or preparation of the cases in which a witness/collaborator of justice is to give evidence.

F. Gathering of financial information

The gathering of financial information to detect financial networks linked to terrorist groups and their investments, including exchanges of information between law enforcement and regulatory bodies, is a part of all strategic approaches to combating terrorism. Establishing national financial intelligence units is part of the capacity-building initiative that must be encouraged.

---

[95]K. Dedel, *Witness Intimidation* ….

[96]Although it is not hard to understand how it may be necessary for the authorities to provide an incentive for cooperation, this must be done cautiously. The presence of certain incentives can in fact compromise the value of the testimony or its credibility.

[97]International Institute of Higher Studies in Criminal Sciences, Monitoring Centre on Organized Crime and European Police Office, *Harmonisation of Witness Protection Legislation: final proposal of the ISISC-OPCO-EUROPOL working group on minimum requirements for potential legislation at European Union Level*, explanatory report (Siracusa, Italy, 2005).

The successful investigation and prosecution of terrorism financing require the quick identification of relevant information from banks, other financial institutions and commercial or other businesses. The tracing and confiscation of assets, both within a jurisdiction and internationally, are made difficult by the complexity of the banking and financial sector. Technological advances are complicating those efforts. Because many such transactions are transnational, changes to bilateral treaties or national legal frameworks are required to allow for the lawful and expeditious exchange of that information across borders between prosecution services or between other law enforcement authorities. In that regard, the existence of unregulated offshore centres presents some practical problems from the point of view of international cooperation among prosecution services. Difficulties are frequently encountered in dealing with the differences in company law and other regulatory norms involved. There are also issues with cyberpayments, "virtual banks" operating in underregulated offshore jurisdictions and shell companies operating outside of the territory of the offshore centres.

The international community has acted on many fronts to respond to the growing complexity and the international nature of the rapidly evolving methods of money-laundering and financing of terrorism. The emphasis has been on promoting international cooperation and establishing a coordinated and effective international regime to combat money-laundering and counter financing of terrorism. The specific obligations of countries in relation to that regime vary depending on their adherence to various treaties. Those obligations are quite complex and can overwhelm countries with limited resources and relatively underdeveloped financial, legal and regulatory institutions.

Within that global regime, because of the relative ease with which proceeds of crime and terrorist funds can be moved around the world, countries with weak mechanisms to counter money-laundering and counter the financing of terrorism are left especially vulnerable to criminal activities. A State must now have an effective national regime in order to avoid having its financial institutions and businesses targeted by money-launderers, terrorist supporters and other criminals. Furthermore, the international regime to counter money-laundering and counter the financing of terrorism is only as strong as its weakest links, and the countries which constitute weak links in that international chain of control are more likely to be targeted by criminals and terrorists.

Participants at the Organization for Security and Cooperation in Europe Expert Workshop on Enhancing Legal Cooperation in Criminal Matters Related to Terrorism suggested the adoption of a non-conviction-based civil forfeiture regime as well as direct methods of execution of mutual legal assistance requests for restraining terrorist assets.[98]

A number of emerging practices in this area are worth considering for strengthening the capacity of the police to intercept criminal assets and to prevent the financing of terrorism,[99] including the following:

- The use of investigative strategies that target the assets of organized crime and terrorist groups through interconnected financial investigations;
- The development of arrangements and a capacity to engage in active and ongoing exchanges of relevant financial intelligence information and analyses;

---

[98]Organization for Security and Cooperation in Europe, Overview of the OSCE Expert Workshop on Enhancing Legal Cooperation in Criminal Matters Relating to Terrorism, Vienna, April 2005.

[99]Group of Eight, "G8 best practice principles on tracing, freezing and confiscation of assets", 2004, available at www.usdoj.gov/criminal/cybercrime/g82004/G8_Best_Practices_on_Tracing.pdf.

- Initiating confiscation or forfeiture of assets proceedings that are independent from other criminal proceedings;

- Establishing methods to mitigate the onus of proof regarding the illicit origin of assets;

- Entering into bilateral or other agreements for sharing assets among countries involved in the tracing, freezing and confiscation of assets originating from organized crime activities.

G. Community engagement

The role of the police in preventing terrorism can be greatly supported by the quality of the relationship it maintains with the local population and with the various ethnic and cultural communities involved. Good relationships can lead to cooperation.

Some countries have placed the police under statutory obligation to promote equality and prevent racial discrimination in carrying out its functions. A variety of methods can be used to help the police improve its relations with ethnic and other potentially vulnerable community groups. Those methods include recruiting members of underrepresented minority groups in the police and ensuring that they have equal opportunities for progression in their careers; training the police in cultural diversity and in policing a diverse society; establishing frameworks for dialogue and cooperation between the police and members of minority groups; and giving police access to interpreters and others who can facilitate communication between the police and members of minority groups.

In some cases, the police can actively engage in a dialogue with various community groups or discuss with them their role in the prevention of terrorism. Many community groups will welcome the opportunity to share with the police some of their concerns about the perceived detrimental impact of various counter-terrorism measures on their lives.

The media can also play an important role in helping the police communicate more honestly and more effectively with the public at large and with minority groups. The police must develop good relationships with the media and must communicate with the media in a manner that does not perpetuate hostility or prejudice towards members of certain groups.

H. International law enforcement cooperation

Because of the dynamic nature of terrorism and transnational crime, States must constantly refine their cooperation strategies in order to achieve integrated, cooperative and strategic approaches to the investigation and prosecution of crimes across borders. International cooperation in all relevant fields is indispensable in the fight against terrorism. The most important form of international cooperation is arguably that which takes place between law enforcement agencies.[100] Such international cooperation requires national efforts to comply with new international standards, encourage convergence and compatibility of national legislation, introduce complex procedural reforms, generally develop a much greater investigative capacity at the national level and strengthen the capacity to cooperate at the international level.

---

[100]Adel Maged, "International legal cooperation: an essential tool in the war against terrorism", *Terrorism and the Military: International Legal Implications*, W. P. Heere, ed. (The Hague, Asser Press, 2003), p. 157.

The global instruments against terrorism and the Organized Crime Convention and the Convention against Corruption provide a strong basis for international law enforcement cooperation and suggest some of the elements that must be developed as part of a national capacity for effective investigation and prosecution of such crimes.

Challenges in law enforcement collaboration

In cases involving transnational offences, States with jurisdiction need to coordinate their respective investigations in order to more effectively target terrorist groups and their international activities. Coordination of cross-border investigations and prosecutions is still rare and tends to require considerable preparation through formal channels.

The importance of operational cooperation across borders among law enforcement agencies investigating and prosecuting terrorist crimes and conspiracies is addressed in a number of international instruments.[101] Nevertheless, practical problems in the organization of joint investigations include the lack of common standards and accepted practices, the actual supervision of the investigation, the prevention of intelligence leaks and the absence of mechanisms for quickly solving these problems.[102]

When a case requires international cooperation, national differences in the law regulating police powers, the use of special investigation techniques, the use of collaborators and informants or the admissibility of certain types of evidence can seriously hinder law enforcement collaboration. Major efforts have been made, through the implementation of the Organized Crime Convention and other international cooperation initiatives to identify such obstacles and remedy the situation. These efforts are also relevant to the prevention of terrorist acts, and their use by law enforcement and intelligence agencies within the framework of ongoing cooperation has drawn some close attention.[103]

Cooperation in the confiscation of terrorism- or crime-related assets

Confiscations within a jurisdiction and international confiscations are made difficult by the complexities of the banking and financial sector and by technological advances. The Convention on Psychotropic Substances of 1971, the United Nations Convention against Illicit Traffic in Narcotic Drugs and Psychotropic Substances of 1988, the Organized Crime Convention, the Convention against Corruption and the International Convention for the Suppression of the Financing of Terrorism contain provisions on the tracing, freezing, seizure and confiscation of instrumentalities and proceeds of crime. Other international efforts to counter money-laundering and the financing of terrorism are based on the FATF Forty Recommendations on Money-Laundering and Nine Special Recommendations on Terrorist Financing and the Basel Committee on Banking Supervision.

---

[101]Article 19 of the Organized Crime Convention requires States parties to consider concluding bilateral or multilateral agreements or arrangements whereby, in relation to matters that are the subject of investigations, prosecutions or judicial proceedings in one or more States, the competent authorities concerned may establish joint investigative bodies. See also similar language in article 49 of the Convention against Corruption.

[102]See T. Schalken, "On joint investigation teams, Europol and supervision of their joint actions", *European Journal of Crime, Criminal Law and Criminal Justice*, vol. 10, No. 1 (2002), pp. 70-82.

[103]The European Court of Human Rights has endorsed the use of such techniques in the fight against terrorism (*Klass and Others v. Germany*) and, within the Council of Europe, a draft recommendation of the Committee of Ministers to member States that seeks to promote the use of special investigative techniques in relation to serious crime, including terrorism, is being drafted. See P. De Koster, "Part 1: analytical report", *Terrorism: Special Investigation Techniques* (Strasbourg, Council of Europe Publishing, 2005), pp. 7-43.

These international legal instruments are meant to ensure that each party adopts such legislative and other measures as may be necessary to trace, identify, freeze, seize and confiscate criminal assets, manage those assets and extend the widest possible cooperation to other States parties in relation to tracing, freezing, seizing or confiscating proceeds of crime. Cooperating States must also possess a similar capability with respect to assets of licit or illicit origin that are used or are to be used for the financing of terrorism.

The implementation of effective measures to counter the financing of terrorism remains a priority for the international community. The International Convention for the Suppression of the Financing of Terrorism requires States parties to engage in wide-ranging cooperation with other States parties and to provide them with legal assistance in the matters covered by the Convention.

The Lyon Group established by the Group of Eight has put forward a set of best practice principles on the tracing, freezing and confiscation of crime-related assets, including assets related to terrorism.[100] Those principles underscore the need for multidisciplinary cooperation between legal, law enforcement, and financial and accountancy experts within and across jurisdictions, and they underline the need for specialized competent authorities to deal with complex cooperation issues.

A number of countries, including Belgium, Ireland and the United Kingdom, have established specialized units to deal with complex confiscation cooperation issues, and an informal network has been established among those units to facilitate their work.

International cooperation can also be substantially facilitated by the development of equitable arrangements for the sharing of forfeited assets and confiscated proceeds of crime. The Organized Crime Convention and the Convention against Corruption contain provisions in that regard.[104]

Coordination of investigations across borders

In cases where terrorist conspiracies occur in several countries at the same time, or when transnational terrorist groups are involved, States with jurisdiction usually find it important to coordinate their investigations, prosecutions and mutual assistance measures to effectively target these groups and their international activities.

The establishment of joint investigative teams represents a major new trend in the development of an effective capacity to investigate and prosecute transnational crimes, including terrorism. It offers one of the most promising new forms of international cooperation against organized crime, corruption and terrorism, even though legal issues, as well as issues of attitude and trust among law enforcement agencies, or even procedural questions still require close attention.

There are also practical problems in the organization and operation of joint investigations, including the lack of common standards and accepted practices, issues around the supervision of the investigation, and the absence of mechanisms for quickly solving these problems. For joint investigative teams to become an effective tool for international

---

[104]United Nations Convention against Transnational Organized Crime, article 14; United Nations Convention against Corruption, chapter V, articles 51-59.

cooperation, States must put in place the required legal framework, both at the national and international levels, although such a framework need not necessarily be very complicated.

A few States members of the European Union have created joint investigation teams to deal with potential terrorist activities and other complex criminal cases requiring international investigation and coordinated law enforcement action. The teams are composed of magistrates and police officers from two or more countries who act as judicial police with powers to carry out searches, interrogations and telephone interceptions within the participating countries.

Exchange of information and intelligence

Once a relationship of confidence and trust has been established between law enforcement agencies, they can engage in ongoing exchanges of information and intelligence. Several agencies have entered into formal information- and intelligence-sharing agreements. Some do so within the framework of international structures such as INTERPOL and Europol, two non-operational organizations whose primary focus is to provide channels for information exchange among law enforcements agencies. Some of those arrangements remain superficial and have yet to produce appreciable results, while others are more promising. Providing real-time access to databases is still rare, as is the linkage of databases, despite the availability of encryption and other technologies allowing agencies to share such information securely. The data do not always circulate freely within a State, let alone across international borders, and there are numerous outstanding issues concerning privacy and the confidentiality of information.

International law enforcement cooperation can be enhanced through the development of more effective systems of information sharing at the regional and global levels on significant trends, criminal patterns, the activities and organization of criminal groups and their respective linkages. The development of regional or subregional databases can also be considered. Mechanisms and processes that take advantage of advances in communication and data storage technologies should be used whenever possible to support exchange mechanisms for the sharing of criminal records and other criminal justice data between States.

In many instances, international law enforcement cooperation is hindered by the absence of clear channels of communication. In other instances, channels exist, but their inefficiency prevents the timely exchange of both operational information (useful in responding to specific offences, offenders or criminal groups) and general information (on criminal networks, trafficking trends and patterns, the extent of known criminal activity in a particular sector and typical modus operandi).

In many States, immense progress has been achieved at the national level in terms of securely sharing criminal records and other data among law enforcement agencies in real time and with the appropriate human rights safeguards. The most significant obstacle to the international exchange of law enforcement data is the lack of the necessary national and international legislative frameworks to support lawful and effective exchanges of data while protecting the privacy of the individuals involved.

In some instances, the sharing of data will continue to be problematic. For example, it is clear that the sharing of data on asylum seekers is often not advisable unless there is a legislated national framework to guide related law enforcement practices. UNHCR, recognizing the fact that the sharing of data between States is crucial in combating terrorism, has made the following recommendations:

> States should, though, also take into account the well-established principle that information on asylum-seekers should not be shared with the country of origin. This could endanger the safety of the bona fide asylum-seeker and/or family members remaining in the country of origin. Best State practice indeed incorporates a strict confidentiality policy. Should it exceptionally be deemed necessary to contact the authorities in the country of origin, in case there is suspicion of terrorist involvement and the required information may only be obtained from these authorities, there should be no disclosure of the fact that the individual has applied for asylum.[34]

Some progress has been made at the bilateral, subregional and regional levels to ensure that current exchange mechanisms fulfil the requirements for law enforcement cooperation while providing all the necessary safeguards for the protection of personal data and individual privacy rights. For example, the European Schengen Information System allows participating national law enforcement agencies to share data on many key issues with their colleagues in other countries almost instantaneously. For most observers, the strength of the arrangements enabled by the Schengen conventions lies in the fact that they allow for highly practical law enforcement cooperation and information exchange at a level that is unique in the world. Europol also produces annual situation reports on organized crime based on the compilation of data provided by all member States. A long-term goal is the establishment of compatible criminal intelligence systems among Member States and the sharing of criminal intelligence data through secure computer networks with controlled access. That process may include setting up a database of pending investigations, making it possible to prevent overlaps between investigations and to involve several competent authorities in the same investigation.

For example, in January 2007, the Committee of Ministers of the Council of Europe recommended that Member States use, in accordance with national law, INTERPOL's three main counter-terrorism tools: a global police communications system called the "I-24/7"; databases containing essential police information (including names, stolen vehicles, stolen travel documents and DNA and fingerprint data); and real-time operational support for police services via the command and coordination centre at the General Secretariat.[105]

International cooperation for witness protection

Because many terrorist groups operate across borders, the threat that they represent to witnesses and collaborators of justice is not confined by national borders. Physical and psychological intimidation of witnesses and their relatives can take place in different locations/jurisdictions. Furthermore, at times, witnesses may need to move to another country or return to their own country during lengthy criminal proceedings. Finally, there are cases in which a State, because of the size of its territory, its lack of means or other circumstances, may not be able to ensure the safety of witnesses. Given such cases, international cooperation in the field of protection of witnesses and their relatives has become a necessary component of normal cooperation between prosecution services. Furthermore, international cooperation may also be required at times in order to protect interpreters, the prosecutors and other judicial and correctional personnel.

---

[105]Council of Europe, Recommendation CM/Rec(2007)1 of the Committee of Ministers to member States regarding cooperation against terrorism between the Council of Europe and its member States, and the International Criminal Police Organization (ICPO-Interpol), adopted by the Committee of Ministers on 18 January 2007.

To ensure greater international cooperation in offering effective witness protection at home or across borders, law enforcement and prosecution agencies often need to develop arrangements with other jurisdictions for the safe examination of witnesses at risk of intimidation or retaliation.[106]

Developing a capacity to protect witnesses and even relocate them in another country must often be considered. Article 24, paragraph 3, of the Organized Crime Convention requires States parties to consider entering into agreements or arrangements with other States for the relocation of witnesses.

In Europe, a major effort has been made to develop legal instruments establishing common criteria for the design and implementation of a set of effective legal and practical protection measures and assistance programmes for different categories of witnesses, victims and collaborators of justice. The objective is to develop such instruments while preserving an acceptable balance between the protection measures and the human rights and fundamental freedoms of all parties involved. There is no legally binding European legal instrument that specifically and comprehensively deals with witness protection.[107] However, a number of significant recommendations of the Committee of Ministers of the Council of Europe have been adopted to deal specifically with witness protection and the rights of witnesses.[108]

In general, the following measures have been found to support international collaboration in the field of witness protection:

- Cooperation in evaluating the threat against a witness or victim;

- Prompt communication of information concerning potential threats and risks;

- Mutual assistance in relocating witnesses and ensuring their ongoing protection;[109]

- Protection of witnesses who are returning to a foreign country in order to testify and collaboration in the safe repatriation of such witnesses;

- Use of modern means of telecommunications to facilitate the simultaneous examination of protected witnesses while safeguarding the rights of the defence;

- Establishing regular communication channels between managers of witness protection programmes;

- Providing technical assistance and encouraging the exchange of trainers and training programmes for officials in the field of victim protection;

---

[106]For some examples of what is usually covered in such arrangements, see United Nations Office on Drugs and Crime, *Good Practices for the Protection of Witnesses in Criminal Proceedings Involving Organized Crime* (New York, 2008), pp. 82-84.

[107]For a summary of the various European legal instruments developed, see Stjepan Gluščic and others, *Protecting Witnesses of Serious Crime: Training Manual for Law Enforcement and Judiciary* (Strasbourg, Council of Europe Publishing, 2006), pp. 38-48. See also Council of Europe, *The Fight against Terrorism: Council of Europe Standards*, 2nd ed. (Strasbourg, Council of Europe Publishing, 2004); and Council of Europe, specific terms of reference for the Committee of Experts on the Protection of Witnesses and Collaborators of Justice, adopted in May 2004, available at the website of the Council of Europe at www.coe.int.

[108]See, for example, Council of Europe, Recommendation Rec(2005)9 of the Committee of Ministers to member States on the protection of witnesses and collaborators of justice, adopted by the Committee of Ministers on 20 April 2005; see also Council of Europe, explanatory report to recommendation Rec(2005)9 of the Committee of Ministers to member States on the protection of witnesses and collaborators of justice, 2005.

[109]See "Witness protection", in Council of Europe, *Combating Organised Crime* ..., pp. 15-42. International cooperation in this area, as noted by a best practice survey conducted by the Council of Europe, "is highly important, since many Member States are too small to guarantee safety for witnesses at risk who are relocated within their borders" (p. 15).

- Developing cost-sharing agreements for joint victim protection initiatives;
- Developing agreements and protocols for the exchange of witnesses who are prisoners.

Europol has developed two documents: "Basic principles of European Union police co-operation in the field of witness protection" and "Common criteria for taking a witness into a protection programme". Europol also offers training each year on witness protection and the handling of informants.

Small States often face unique difficulties in offering effective protection to witnesses and can benefit from cooperating with each other in developing their witness protection capacity.[110]

I. Extraordinary measures

All measures taken by law enforcement agencies to combat terrorism must be lawful. In that respect, some specific law enforcement activities against terrorism have raised serious concerns and human rights issues. Some States have engaged in extraordinary law enforcement measures that are problematic, including shooting without warning, targeted killings and extraordinary renditions. These so-called "exceptional measures" have underscored the need to ensure that, in adopting measures aimed at preventing and controlling acts of terrorism, States adhere to the rule of law, including the basic principles, standards and obligations of criminal and international law that define the boundaries of permissible and legitimate State action against terrorism and the various forms of serious crime in which terrorists and other criminal groups are involved. States may never act in breach of peremptory norms of international law or in breach of international humanitarian law.

All States have a positive obligation to ensure that their territory is not used to transfer persons to places where they are likely to be killed or subjected to torture, including by taking all practical steps to determine whether there are grounds to believe that actions taken by foreign entities in their territory involve such practices.

A State's international responsibility may be engaged if State actors commit internationally wrongful acts, bring assistance or aid to another State in the commission of a wrongful act, acquiesce to such wrongful conduct or fail to take measures to prevent such acts from occurring on its territory. When such wrongful acts have taken place, the State must undertake prompt and effective measures to investigate those occurrences, prosecute those responsible for the violation and ensure that the victims are adequately compensated.

Shooting without warning and shooting on sight

The need to take protective measures against the phenomenon of suicide bombers has driven certain countries to tolerate exceptions to internationally recognized human rights.

---

[110]Member States of the Caribbean Community, for example, have established the Agreement establishing the Regional Justice Protection Programme (1999), outlining the need to prevent any interference in the administration of justice through the intimidation or elimination of witnesses, jurors, judicial and legal officers and law enforcement personnel and their associates. The Agreement also provides for the establishment of a regional centre to administer the cooperation programme.

The Special Rapporteur on the promotion and protection of human rights and fundamental freedoms while countering terrorism expressed concern about legal strategies
employed by many States to extend the powers of policemen to take action against potential suicide bombers. He reiterated that the use of lethal force by law enforcement officers
must be regulated within the framework of human rights law and its strict standard of
necessity. The "defence of necessity" that is invoked by law enforcement officials applies
only when there is an imminent danger.

In several of his communications with Governments, the Special Rapporteur on extrajudicial, summary or arbitrary executions has drawn attention to the increasing reluctance
to respect the right to life as a non-derogable human right.[111] In his view, the rhetoric of
"shoot-to-kill" serves only to displace clear legal standards with a vaguely defined licence
to kill, risking confusion among law enforcement officers, endangering innocent persons
and rationalizing mistakes, while avoiding the genuinely difficult challenges that are posed
by the relevant threat.

The Code of Conduct for Law Enforcement Officials, adopted by the General Assembly
in its resolution 34/169 of 17 December 1979, and the Basic Principles on the Use of
Force and Firearms by Law Enforcement Officials,[112] adopted at the Eighth United Nations
Congress on the Prevention of Crime and the Treatment of Offenders, succinctly stress
the limited role of lethal force in all enforcement operations. Principle 9 of the Basic
Principles on the Use of Force and Firearms by Law Enforcement Officials states that in
any event, intentional lethal use of firearms may only be made when strictly unavoidable
in order to protect life. These instruments are adequate also with respect to the prevention of suicide attacks as a form of terrorism. Principle 10 of the Basic Principles states
the following:

> Law enforcement officials shall identify themselves as such and give a clear warning
> of their intent to use firearms, with sufficient time for the warning to be observed,
> unless to do so would unduly place the law enforcement officials at risk or would
> create a risk of death or serious harm to other persons, or would be clearly inap-
> propriate or pointless in the circumstances of the incident.

Targeted killings

The right to life is non-derogable, and lethal force taken in the context of counter-terrorism
must be necessary and proportional. The Human Rights Commission has expressed concerns with respect to the alleged use of the so-called "targeted killings" of suspected terrorists.[113] In some cases, the practice appears to have been used in part as a deterrent or
punishment, thus raising issues related to article 6, paragraph 1, of the International
Covenant on Civil and Political Rights, which states the following: "Every human being
has the inherent right to life. This right shall be protected by law. No one shall be arbitrarily deprived of his life."

---

[111] Report of the Special Rapporteur on extrajudicial, summary or arbitrary executions (E/CN.4/2006/53,
paras. 44-54).

[112]*Eighth United Nations Congress on the Prevention of Crime and the Treatment of Offenders, Havana, 27
August-7 September 1990: report prepared by the Secretariat* (United Nations publication, Sales No. E.91.IV.2),
chap. I, sect. B.2, annex.

[113]Edward J. Flynn, "Counter-terrorism and human rights: the view from the United Nations", *European
Human Rights Law Review*, No. 1, 2005, p. 34.

Prohibition of extra-legal, arbitrary and summary executions

(from the Principles on the Effective Prevention and Investigation of Extra-legal, Arbitrary and Summary Executions[a])

"1. Governments shall prohibit by law all extra-legal, arbitrary and summary executions and shall ensure that any such executions are recognized as offences under their criminal laws, and are punishable by appropriate penalties which take into account the seriousness of such offences. Exceptional circumstances including a state of war or threat of war, internal political instability or any other public emergency may not be invoked as a justification of such executions. Such executions shall not be carried out under any circumstances including, but not limited to, situations of internal armed conflict, excessive or illegal use of force by a public official or other person acting in an official capacity or by a person acting at the instigation, or with the consent or acquiescence of such person, and situations in which deaths occur in custody. This prohibition shall prevail over decrees issued by governmental authority.

"2. In order to prevent extra-legal, arbitrary and summary executions, Governments shall ensure strict control, including a clear chain of command over all officials responsible for apprehension, arrest, detention, custody and imprisonment, as well as those officials authorized by law to use force and firearms.

"3. Governments shall prohibit orders from superior officers or public authorities authorizing or inciting other persons to carry out any such extra-legal, arbitrary or summary executions. All persons shall have the right and the duty to defy such orders. Training of law enforcement officials shall emphasize the above provisions.

"4. Effective protection through judicial or other means shall be guaranteed to individuals and groups who are in danger of extra-legal, arbitrary or summary executions, including those who receive death threats."

[a]Principles on the Effective Prevention and Investigation of Extra-legal, Arbitrary and Summary Executions (Economic and Social Council resolution 1989/65, annex) paras. 1-4.

In a case where an extra-legal or arbitrary execution is suspected, there must be a thorough, prompt and impartial investigation. The purpose of such an investigation is to determine the cause, manner and time of death, the person responsible, and any pattern or practice which may have brought about that death. It must include an adequate autopsy, as well as the collection and analysis of all physical and documentary evidence and statements from witnesses. Furthermore, governments must ensure that persons identified by the investigation as having participated in extra-legal, arbitrary or summary executions in any territory under their jurisdiction are brought to justice. Governments must either bring such persons to justice or cooperate to extradite them to other countries wishing to exercise jurisdiction. This principle applies irrespective of who and where the perpetrators or the victims are, their nationalities, or where the offence was committed.[114]

---

[114]Principles on the Effective Prevention and Investigation of Extra-legal, Arbitrary and Summary Executions (Economic and Social Council resolution 1989/65, annex).

IV. Role of prosecutors

The effective prosecution of terrorist offences, wherever they are committed and wherever the perpetrator takes refuge, is crucial in order to deny safe haven to the perpetrators of such crimes. In the case of international or transnational crime and terrorism, this raises the issue of establishing and exercising jurisdictions, the questions of prosecutorial capacity and independence and the issue of the need to address various obstacles to international cooperation in the prosecution of terrorist offences.

The role of prosecutors in prosecuting terrorist offences is more or less the same as their role in the prosecution of any criminal offence. However, in the case of international crimes or any offence that has a transnational aspect, jurisdictional issues and various impediments to effective international cooperation often complicate matters.

The two main mechanisms supporting international cooperation among prosecutors are extradition and mutual legal assistance. These mechanisms are based on a number of legal foundations, including bilateral and multilateral agreements or arrangements. All these mechanisms are evolving rapidly to keep pace with new criminal methods and criminal exploitation of new technologies. Their evolution reflects the new determination of States to work more closely with each other to face the growing threats of organized crime, corruption and terrorism.[115]

A. Independence of the prosecution

To maintain the integrity of the prosecution function and uphold the rule of law, States must take measures to ensure the integrity and independence of prosecution services. Political and other forms of interference with the impartial and fair execution of the prosecution function are in direct contradiction with the principle of the rule of law.

The quality of the legal training offered to professional prosecutors varies greatly from State to State. As is reiterated in the preamble to the Guidelines on the Role of Prosecutors, it continues to be important for States to ensure that prosecutors possess the professional qualifications required for the accomplishment of their functions, through improved methods of recruitment and legal and professional training, and through the provision of all necessary means for the proper performance of their role in combating criminality.[116]

---

[115]Y. Dandurand, "Strategies and practical measures to strengthen the capacity of prosecution services in dealing with transnational organized crime, terrorism and corruption", *Crime, Law and Social Change*, vol. 47, Nos. 4-5 (2007), pp. 225-246; Y. Dandurand, G. Colombo and N. Passas, "Measures and mechanisms to strengthen international cooperation among prosecution services", *Crime, Law and Social Change*, vol. 47, Nos. 4-5 (2007), pp. 261-289.

[116] Guidelines on the Role of Prosecutors (*Eighth United Nations Congress on the Prevention of Crime and the Treatment of Offenders, Havana, 27 August-7 September 1990: report prepared by the Secretariat* (United Nations publication, Sales No. E.91.IV.2), chap. I, sect. C.26, annex); available at http://www2.ohchr.org/english/law/pdf/prosecutors.pdf.

B.   Role of prosecutors in upholding the rule of law

The basic role of prosecutors varies considerably among legal systems, as does the extent of their power and authority. In particular, prosecutors may play a more or less active role in the actual investigation of crime, depending on national law, and as a result, their respective relationship with the police can vary from country to country. In some jurisdictions, a large proportion of the prosecutions are carried out by police officers. In some countries, prosecutors are elected, while in others they are appointed.

The essence of the role of prosecutors in upholding the rule of law is captured in part by the Guidelines on the Role of Prosecutors, which affirms the following:

> "11.   Prosecutors shall perform an active role in criminal proceedings, including institution of prosecution and, where authorized by law or consistent with local practice, in the investigation of crime, supervision over the legality of these investigations, supervision of the execution of court decisions and the exercise of other functions as representatives of the public interest.

> "12.   Prosecutors shall, in accordance with the law, perform their duties fairly, consistently and expeditiously, and respect and protect human dignity and uphold human rights, thus contributing to ensuring due process and the smooth functioning of the criminal justice system."[117]

Prosecution services are a vital part of States' efforts to affirm the rule of law through the fair, consistent, impartial and effective enforcement of the law. Without the commitment of prosecutors to human rights and to upholding the rule of law, the criminal justice system and governing institutions risk falling into disrepute and losing credibility and moral authority.[118]

Prosecutors are also important guarantors of the rule of law inasmuch as they accept the role of combating impunity and ensuring the lawfulness of State actions. By tackling impunity for human rights abuses wherever they arise, prosecutors not only reinforce respect for the rule of law at the national level, but they also help consolidate the principle of rule of law at the international level.

Prosecutors must remain vigilant and ensure that the actions of the police, corrections and other law enforcement authorities are lawful and respectful of human rights. They do so partly by bringing to the attention of the courts any instance of unlawful or corrupt behaviour by agents of the State or other officials in positions of authority and by vigorously prosecuting such offenders to the full extent of the law. In cases involving the corruption of public officials, the role of prosecutors is particularly important and delicate.

The debilitating effects of corruption on the rule of law are all too obvious. Corruption within the justice system itself is a concern, as are the implications of such corruption for upholding the rule of law and preserving the integrity of the criminal investigation and prosecution processes. Corruption not only affects the credibility and effectiveness of a justice system in a general sense; it also compromises international cooperation in criminal matters, defeats coordination efforts and places witnesses, victims and justice officials at risk. Preventing corruption is one of the most important ways in which prosecutors

---

[117]Ibid., paras. 11-12.

[118]Y. Dandurand, "The role of prosecutors in promoting and strengthening the rule of law", *Crime, Law and Social Change*, vol. 47, Nos. 4-5 (2007), pp. 247-259.

protect the rule of law and the integrity of social and economic institutions. Article 15 of the Guidelines on the Role of Prosecutors specifies that prosecutors shall give due attention to the prosecution of crimes committed by public officials, particularly corruption, abuse of power, grave violations of human rights and other crimes recognized by international law and, where authorized by law or consistent with local practice, the investigation of such offences.

C. Obligation to extradite or prosecute

The principle of *aut dedere, aut judicare* translates into the alternatives of extradite or prosecute, which is an obligation expressed in the universal instruments against terrorism and is implicit in Security Council resolution 1373 (2001). The principle expresses the common objective of States in fighting serious forms of crime and sets out the alternatives for the requested State whenever the extradition of an individual present in its territory is requested: a State must either hand over the person concerned to the requesting State or try the case itself.

The principle of "extradite or prosecute" requires States to assert their jurisdiction on more traditional bases: the principle of territorial jurisdiction, either ordinary or extended, notably to flag vessels and State-registered aircraft; and the nationality principle, in particular active nationality, establishing the jurisdiction of the State whose national is suspected of committing the offence, but also passive nationality, whereby the State of which the victim is a national has jurisdiction to prosecute the offender. Finally, some conventions allow States to create optional jurisdiction over an alleged offender who is a habitual resident of that State or if the offence involves State interests.

The obligation to prosecute does not, however, mean that an allegation that, following an investigation, is established as unfounded has to be brought before a court. The constitutional law and substantive and procedural rules of the country concerned will determine to what extent the prosecution must be pursued. Nevertheless, the universal instruments require States parties to initiate the prosecution process for a serious offence under domestic law.

D. Extradition

Extradition is the procedure whereby a sovereign State, referred to as the "requested State", agrees to hand over an individual to another sovereign State, referred to as the "requesting State", for prosecution or, if that person has already been tried and convicted, for enforcement of the sentence.

Under the requirement of dual criminality, extradition is possible only when the act is punishable under the law of both the requested and the requesting States. The name of the offence and the elements that make it criminal need not be precisely the same, provided that the fugitive could be punished for the act in both States.[119] For that reason, the criminalization of defined terrorist acts and their incorporation into national criminal law is a central element of the relevant universal legal instruments against terrorism.

---

[119]For a discussion of the implications of dual criminality for international cooperation in relation to terrorist offences, see *Legislative Guide to the Universal Legal Regime against Terrorism* (United Nations publication, Sales No. E.08.V.9), p. 40.

As noted above, when a person accused of having committed a terrorist offence is present in the territory of a State party and the authorities of the State party are satisfied that the circumstances so warrant, the State must, in accordance with its law, take the person into custody or take other measures to enable any criminal or extradition proceedings to be instituted. That is to be done independent of whether the crime was committed on its territory and whether the State has received a request for provisional arrest pending a formal request for extradition. The universal instruments against terrorism do not make the extradition of the offender mandatory but define it as one possible course of action. The obligation to submit the individual to prosecution depends on a decision not to extradite.

States need to continue to enhance their treaty network and modernize their extradition treaties. In many instances, changes to national extradition legislation are required as a procedural or enabling framework in support of the implementation of the relevant international treaties. In cases where a State can extradite in the absence of a treaty, national legislation is often useful as a supplementary, comprehensive and self-standing framework for surrendering fugitives to requesting States. UNODC has prepared a model law on extradition to assist interested Member States in drafting such legislation.[120]

Recent trends in extradition treaties have focused on relaxing the strict application of certain grounds for refusal of extradition requests. In addition, the principle of mutual recognition is increasingly perceived as a means of improving judicial cooperation between countries with different legal systems and replacing cumbersome procedures with swift procedures that recognize the integrity of other legal systems. For example, mutual recognition of arrest warrants, whereby an arrest warrant issued by a competent authority in one State is recognized as valid and is enforced by another State (a practice also referred to as the "backing of warrants"), expedites the extradition process. Several countries now have bilateral arrangements for extradition.

Another example is provided by the European arrest warrant, which since the beginning of 2004 has effectively replaced extradition procedures by a system of surrender between judicial authorities in countries covered by the scheme. The European arrest warrant allows requests for the arrest or surrender of a person to be executed with the minimum of formalities for the purpose of conducting criminal prosecutions, executing custodial sentences or executing detention orders.

Effective extradition casework

The UNODC Informal Expert Working Group on Effective Extradition Casework Practice developed a list of concrete suggestions on how to enhance the effectiveness of extradition casework,[a] including the following suggestions:

• Enable lawful extradition without a treaty wherever appropriate.

• Make an inventory of extradition laws and treaties.

• Ensure extradition laws and treaties are flexible and up to date, including by renegotiating and extending the treaties wherever appropriate.

---

[120]Model Treaty on Extradition, adopted by the General Assembly in its resolution 45/116 of 14 December 1990, and subsequently amended by the General Assembly in its resolution 52/88 of 12 December 1997; *Compendium of United Nations Standards and Norms in Crime Prevention and Criminal Justice* (New York, 2006), pp. 163-173. See also the Revised Manuals on the Model Treaty on Extradition and on the Model Treaty on Mutual Assistance in Criminal Matters (E/CN.15/2004/CRP.11), available at www.unodc.org/pdf/model_treaty_extradition_revised_manual.pdf.

- Reduce or eliminate authentication and certification requirements.
- Enable the temporary surrender of persons sought to the requesting State.
- Enable the consenting surrender of persons sought to the requesting State.
- Reform and simplify double (dual) criminality requirements in domestic laws treaties.
- Restrict offences qualifying as political offences to the essential minimum.
- Relax prohibitions against the extradition of nationals.
- Enable the redetermination of citizenship, amnesty and other status improperly obtained to block extradition.
- Deploy and make appropriate and constructive use of staff located abroad, including criminal justice liaison personnel and consular staff.
- Simplify judicial review and appeals processes relating to extradition orders without prejudicing the fundamental right of the person sought to review or appeal.

[a]Report of the Informal Expert Working Group on Effective Extradition Casework Practice (Vienna, 2004), pp. 8-15, available at http://www.unodc.org/pdf/ewg_report_extraditions_2004.pdf.

Measures to strengthen the rule of law and promote human rights are also directly relevant to enhancing international cooperation in the area of extradition. For example, a State is more likely to cooperate with another State in an extradition case if it has assurances that the accused will have the right to a fair trial and due process.

The Council of Europe Guidelines on Human Rights and the Fight against Terrorism make it explicit that extradition should not be granted if there are serious reasons to believe that the person whose extradition has been requested will be subjected to torture or inhuman or degrading treatment or when that person has suffered or risks suffering denial of justice by the requesting State. In the latter case, there is an important role for prosecutors, who have a duty to establish whether there is indeed a risk of denial of justice or torture. They must also determine whether an extradition request has been submitted for the purpose of prosecuting or punishing a person on account of that person's race, religion, nationality or political opinions.

Several of the universal legal instruments include similar provisions. Article 15 of the International Convention for the Suppression of the Financing of Terrorism provides a good example; it expressly permits States to refuse extradition or mutual legal assistance if there are reasonable grounds that the requesting State is acting for the purpose of prosecuting or punishing a person on prohibited grounds of discrimination.

International refugee law does not preclude the extradition for prosecution purposes of recognized refugees, much less that of asylum seekers. However, extradition should be granted only after the corresponding legal proceedings have been completed and if it has been shown that the extradition is not being requested solely or principally as a means of returning a person to a country for purposes which in fact amount to persecution.

Articles in universal instruments negotiated since the adoption in 1997 of the International Convention for the Suppression of Terrorist Bombings provide that for the purposes of extradition or mutual legal assistance, none of the defined offences shall be regarded as a political offence, an offence connected with a political offence or an offence inspired by political motives. Historically, refusal of requests for international cooperation on those grounds had created obstacles to extradition and mutual assistance with respect to terrorism-related offences, almost all of which are connected with political activity or inspired by a political motive. It was possible to eliminate the "political offence exception" because accompanying legislative articles ensured that there was no obligation to provide cooperation in cases in which there were substantial grounds to believe that an extradition request was being made for the purpose of persecuting a person on account of that person's race, religion, nationality, ethnic origin or political opinion.

UNHCR recommends that the retention of this safeguard be mandatory rather than optional. In the case of a pending asylum procedure, it is recommended that further consideration of the asylum claim be deferred until the proceedings in the extradition process enable an informed decision to be made on whether exclusion from refugee status is justified. If the asylum-seeker is found to be excludable, a decision on the extradition could be taken without reassessing the persecution element. If the asylum-seeker is not excluded and it is assessed that extradition would, indeed, amount to return to persecution, prosecution in the country of asylum is, in the view of UNHCR, the appropriate response, based on the principle aut *dedere, aut judicare*.[34]

E. Mutual legal assistance

With the globalization of crime, national authorities increasingly need the assistance of authorities in other countries for the successful investigation, prosecution and punishment of wrongdoers, in particular those who have committed international terrorist offences. In its resolution 1373 (2001), the Security Council decided that all States should afford one another the greatest measure of assistance in connection with criminal investigations or criminal proceedings relating to the financing or support of terrorist acts, including assistance in obtaining evidence in their possession necessary for the proceedings. That provision is binding for all States, including States that have not ratified all or some of the universal counter-terrorism instruments.

To achieve that objective, States most frequently make use of bilateral and multilateral treaties on mutual legal assistance in criminal matters, in addition to existing informal cooperation mechanisms. Those instruments assist the work of criminal justice officials in several ways. For example, they enable the authorities to obtain evidence abroad, through a procedure that is admissible under their domestic law, in order to summon witnesses, trace individuals, secure the production of documents and other evidentiary items and issue warrants.[121]

The current trend in international cooperation mechanisms is to favour arrangements that do the following:

- Allow direct transmission between criminal justice authorities, including central authorities, without use of the diplomatic channel, of requests for mutual assistance and expedite the sending and service of procedural documents;
- Require compliance with formalities and procedures indicated and deadlines set by the requesting State party;

---

[121] See the Model Treaty on Mutual Assistance in Criminal Matters (General Assembly resolution 45/117, annex, and resolution 53/112, annex I. See also the Revised Manuals on the Model Treaty on Extradition and on the Model Treaty on Mutual Assistance in Criminal Matters. A Model Law on Mutual Assistance in Criminal Matters (2007) is available at www.unodc.org/pdf/model_law_on_mutual_sistance.pdf.

- Facilitate the cross-border use of technical equipment (for observation purposes) and the interception of communications;

- Authorize controlled deliveries and allow covert investigations to take place across borders;

- Encourage the establishment of joint investigation teams;

- Permit, under certain circumstances, the hearing of witnesses by video or telephone conference;

- Permit the temporary and lawful transfer of persons held in custody for the purposes of investigation.

Offences defined in the universal instruments against terrorism may not, for the purposes of mutual legal assistance, be regarded as political offences, as offences related to political offences or as offences inspired by political motives. Accordingly, a request for mutual assistance based on any such offence may not be refused on the sole ground that it concerns a political offence, an offence connected with a political offence or an offence inspired by political motives.

The mutual legal assistance provisions contained in the universal instruments provide a State party with a legal basis for transmitting to another State party information or evidence that it deems important to combating terrorist offences, even if the other State has not made any request for assistance and is totally unaware of the existence of such information or evidence. Indeed, Security Council resolution 1373 (2001) obliges States to offer each other such assistance.

At the operational level, designating a single central authority for all incoming and outgoing legal assistance and extradition requests is crucial to international cooperation in criminal matters. In this way, a State can coordinate its own requests for assistance and stand ready to respond expeditiously to requests from other States. Increasingly, mutual legal assistance treaties, such as the Organized Crime Convention and the Convention against Corruption, require that States parties designate a central authority (generally the Ministry of Justice) to which requests can be sent, thus providing an alternative to diplomatic channels. Nevertheless, the role of the central authorities need not necessarily be an exclusive one. Direct exchanges of information and cooperation, to the extent permitted by domestic law, should also be encouraged.

As an outcome to the meeting of the United Nations Office for Drug Control and Crime Prevention Informal Expert Working Group on Mutual Legal Assistance Casework Best Practice, held in Vienna in December 2001,[122] the Working Group recommended a number of best practices that States can use to facilitate mutual legal assistance:

- Minimizing the grounds upon which assistance may be refused (e.g. finding ways to minimize the consequences of the principle of *ne bis in idem* as grounds for refusal);

- Reducing limitations on the use of evidence in response to a request for mutual assistance and streamlining the grounds upon which and the process whereby limitations are imposed;

---

[122] Report of the Informal Expert Working Group on Mutual Legal Assistance Casework Best Practice (Vienna, 2001), available at http://www.unodc.org/pdf/lap_mlaeg_report_final.pdf.

- Making efforts to ensure that requests are executed in compliance with procedures and formalities specified by the requesting State to ensure that the request achieves its purpose;

- Improving the protection of confidential data and information;

- Ensuring the confidentiality of requests for assistance received when possible and, when not possible, advising the requesting State that its request may not be kept confidential;

- Making efforts to ensure that requests are executed within the deadlines specified by the requesting State;

- Coordinating multijurisdictional cases among the jurisdictions involved;

- Ensuring that their legal framework does not provide fortuitous opportunities for third parties to unduly delay cooperation or completely block the execution of a request for assistance on technical grounds.

The Working Group suggested that cooperation could be expedited through the use of alternatives to formal mutual assistance requests, such as informal police channels and communication mechanisms, in particular if evidence is voluntarily given or publicly available, or through the use of joint investigation teams with a capacity to directly transmit and satisfy informal requests for assistance.

The Working Group also identified a number of practical ways to promote international cooperation, including the following:

- Ensure awareness of national legal requirements among foreign officials involved in international cooperation by developing guidelines, simple forms, checklists and procedural guides on requirements;

- Enhance the training of personnel involved in mutual legal assistance through the provision of technical assistance when required, seminars by central authorities and exchanges of personnel between authorities;

- Encourage direct personal contact between officials;

- Encourage the use of liaison magistrates, prosecutors and police officers;

- Interpret the prerequisites to cooperation liberally, in favour of cooperation and to avoid rigid interpretations;

- Consult before rejecting a request for assistance or postponing or imposing conditions on a response to such a request and determine whether the problem that has been identified can be overcome;

- Make use of modern technology to expedite the transmission of requests;

- Optimize language capabilities of central authorities.

The possibility of transferring proceedings in criminal matters from one State to another offers another interesting option upon which to build stronger international cooperation. Such a transfer can be used to increase the likelihood of the success of a prosecution, if for example another State appears to be in a better position to conduct the proceedings. It can also be used to increase the efficiency and effectiveness of the prosecution in a State that is initiating proceedings in lieu of extradition. Finally, it can be a useful method for consolidating the prosecution in one jurisdiction and increasing its efficiency and likelihood of success in cases involving several jurisdictions.

States can simplify their procedures for recognizing court orders relating to freezing, forfeiture and seizure of criminal assets. In the European Union, for example, a set of framework decisions agreed upon in 2001 and 2003 established rules enabling Member States to recognize and execute in their territory a freezing order issued by a judicial authority of another Member State in the context of criminal proceedings.[123]

Article 8 of the 1988 Convention, article 21 of the Organized Crime Convention and article 47 of the Convention against Corruption contain provisions enabling States parties to transfer proceedings where such transfer is in the interests of the proper administration of justice. The United Nations has prepared a Model Treaty on the Transfer of Proceedings in Criminal Matters.[124]

F. Increasing a system's capacity for international cooperation

Criminal justice officials and policymakers should continually seek to enhance their system's capacity to engage in effective international cooperation including by the following actions:

- Developing national policies for international cooperation;

- Ensuring that the relevant bilateral, regional and multilateral treaties are ratified and updated as necessary;

- Reviewing and enhancing their procedural law framework to ensure that it facilitates or at least does not preclude international cooperation;

- Reviewing and enhancing their national law framework to include measures that enable mutual legal assistance and law enforcement cooperation as required by international treaties or multilateral agreements;

- Developing the capacity of existing institutions and agencies to develop, use and respond to requests for mutual legal assistance and information;

- Developing procedures for engaging in mutual legal assistance in criminal matters;

- Reviewing and enhancing their national law framework to enable extradition as required by all treaties to which their State is a party and ensure that the appropriate criminal acts are extraditable, and establishing their legal jurisdiction over those criminal acts;

- Developing national policies and implementing procedures to facilitate the exchange and analysis of information and the protection of sensitive information received through such exchanges;

---

[123]Council of the European Union framework decision 2001/500/JHA of 26 June 2001 on money-laundering, the identification, tracing, freezing, seizing and confiscation of instrumentalities and the proceeds of crime (*Official Journal of the European Communities*, L 182, 5 July 2001); Council of the European Union framework decision 2003/577/JHA of 22 July 2003 on the execution in the European Union of orders freezing property or evidence (*Official Journal of the European Union*, L 196, 2 August 2003). In May 2005, a comprehensive regional framework for international cooperation in such matters was also adopted in the Council of Europe Convention on Laundering, Search, Seizure and Confiscation of the Proceeds from Crime and on the Financing of Terrorism (Council of Europe, *Treaty Series*, No. 198).

[124]General Assembly resolution 45/118, annex.

- Implementing various mechanisms to facilitate international cooperation between the various agencies involved, including central authorities, liaison magistrates of police officers and in the areas of secondments and exchanges of prosecutors and law enforcement officials, networks for collaboration and the exchange of information and information systems
- Developing the capacity of authorities to cooperate at the international level in the protection of victims, their compensation for the harm they suffer, and their safe repatriation when necessary.

V. Role of defence counsel

In securing justice as a basic human right, the Universal Declaration of Human Rights enshrines the key principles of equality before the law, the presumption of innocence, the right to a fair and public hearing by an independent and impartial tribunal, along with all the guarantees necessary for the defence of persons charged with a penal offence. Article 14 of the International Covenant on Civil and Political Rights provides for the minimum fair trial guarantees: the right to be tried without undue delay; the right to a fair and public hearing by a competent, independent and impartial tribunal established by law and to defend oneself in person or through legal assistance of one's own choosing; the right to be informed, if one does not have legal assistance, of the right to such assistance; the right to have legal assistance assigned to one, in any case where the interests of justice so require, without payment; and the right to have adequate time and facilities for the preparation of one's defence and to communicate with counsel of one's own choosing. The Body of Principles for the Protection of All Persons under Any Form of Detention or Imprisonment provides that a detained person shall be entitled to have the assistance of counsel, while the Standard Minimum Rules for the Treatment of Prisoners[125] recommend that legal assistance be assured for prisoners pending adjudication.

These instruments recognize that individuals have a right to legal assistance when their fundamental rights to liberty and life are at stake. The Basic Principles on the Role of Lawyers,[126] adopted by the Eighth United Nations Congress on the Prevention of Crime and the Treatment of Offenders, establishes as its first principle that all persons are entitled to call upon the assistance of a lawyer of their choice to protect and establish their rights and to defend them in all stages of criminal proceedings.

The Basic Principles on the Role of Lawyers place further responsibility upon Governments and the legal profession to ensure access to counsel for everyone, irrespective of their means or background, as a means of ensuring that the right to equality before the law is upheld. As a logical extension, States are required to provide legal aid in the case of indigent defendants. However, the issue of the ability of the State to institute such schemes cannot be ignored. Many States require mandatory assistance by legal counsel in capital cases or cases that involve long prison sentences.

As mentioned above, article 14 of the ICCPR establishes the right of all persons accused of having committed a crime to be tried in their presence and to defend themselves in person or through legal assistance of their own choosing. They also have a right to be informed, if they do not have legal assistance, of the right to obtain legal assistance. Where the interests of justice so require, they have a right to receive free legal assistance.

---

[125]*First United Nations Congress on the Prevention of Crime and the Treatment of Offenders, Geneva, 22 August-3 September 1955: report prepared by the Secretariat* (United Nations publication, Sales No. 1956.IV.4), annex I.A; and Economic and Social Council resolution 2076 (LXII).

[126]Basic Principles on the Role of Lawyers (*Eighth United Nations Congress on the Prevention of Crime and the Treatment of Offenders, Havana, 27 August-7 September 1990: report prepared by the Secretariat* (United Nations publication, Sales No. E.91.IV.2), chap. I, sect. B.3, annex).

The right to counsel

The right to counsel of persons charged with a criminal act is integral to the right to a fair trial and is a fundamental right recognized by the Universal Declaration of Human Rights, the International Covenant on Civil and Political Rights (article 14) and regional human rights treaties and conventions, including the European Convention for the Protection of Human Rights and Fundamental Freedoms[a] (article 6), the American Convention on Human Rights (article 8) and the African Charter on Human and Peoples' Rights[b] (article 7).

Principle 1 of the Basic Principles on the Role of Lawyers states that all persons are entitled to call upon the assistance of a lawyer of their choice to protect and establish their rights and to defend them in all stages of criminal proceedings. Principle 5 requires that all persons detained, arrested or charged be immediately informed of their right to be assisted by a lawyer of their choice. Principle 6 requires that "in all cases which the interests of justice so require, be entitled to have a lawyer of experience and competence commensurate with the nature of the offence assigned to them in order to provide effective legal assistance, without payment by them if they lack sufficient means to pay for such services. Principle 7 requires that all persons who have been detained or arrested be given prompt access to a lawyer, and in any case not later than forty-eight hours from the time of arrest or detention.

Principle 2 of the Basic Principles requires Governments to implement efficient procedures and mechanisms that allow effective and equal access to lawyers and requires that such access be provided to all persons within their territory and subject to their jurisdiction, without distinction of any kind, such as discrimination based on race, colour, ethnic origin, sex, language, religion, political or other opinion, national or social origin, property, birth, economic or other status. Principle 3 states that Governments shall ensure sufficient funding and other resources to provide legal services for the poor and other disadvantaged persons. Professional associations of lawyers are to cooperate in the organization and provision of services, facilities and other resources. The need for confidential communications between lawyer and client is critical to a meaningful exercise of the right to counsel and its attendant lawyer-client relationship. Principle 8 of the Basic Principles requires all persons in custody to be provided with adequate opportunities, time and facilities to be visited by and to communicate and consult with a lawyer, without delay, interception or censorship and in full confidentiality. While such consultations may be observed, they may not be heard. Similarly, principle 22 requires Governments to recognize and respect that all communications and consultations between lawyers and their clients within their professional relationship are confidential.

[a]United Nations, *Treaty Series*, vol. 213, No. 2889.
[b]United Nations, *Treaty Series*, vol. 1520, No. 26363.

A.   Principle of equality of arms

A basic tenet of justice relating to the right to counsel is the principle of equality of arms. The concept encompasses the idea that both parties are treated in a manner ensuring that they have a procedurally equal position during the course of the trial and are in an equal position to make their case.[127] Thus, each party must be afforded a reasonable opportunity to present its case, under conditions that do not place it at a substantial disadvantage vis-à-vis the opposing party.

In criminal trials, where the prosecution has the power of the State behind it, the principle of equality of arms is an essential guarantee of the right to defend oneself. The principle ensures that the defence has a reasonable opportunity to prepare and present its case on a footing equal to that of the prosecution. It encompasses the right to adequate time and facilities to prepare the defence, including the disclosure by the prosecution of material

---

[127]See European Court of Human Rights, judgements in the cases of *Ofner and Hopfinger against Austria* (Applications Nos. 524/59 and 617/59).

information.[128] Equality of arms also includes the right to legal counsel, the right to call and examine witnesses and the right to be present at the trial. The principle would be violated if, for example, the accused was not given access to information necessary for the preparation of the defence, was denied access to expert witnesses or was excluded from an appeal hearing where the prosecutor was present.

The challenge is how to balance the legitimate requirements for the confidentiality of certain informants and the safety of sources with the right of the accused to a fair trial. Practice and jurisprudence show that tribunals recognize the need for the State (prosecution) to protect witnesses and certain information. Nowhere is this more evident than in cases involving terrorists and terrorist organizations. However, blanket permission to the State for such confidentiality would have a detrimental effect on fair trial guarantees. The right approach is for a tribunal, justified by the prosecution, to determine on a case-by-case basis why defence rights should be abridged in this way.

Notice of the right to counsel and the right to choose defence counsel

The accused facing a terrorist criminal trial must be notified of his or her right to be defended by counsel.[129] This right is applicable whether or not the accused has been arrested or detained before trial. In order for the notice to be effective, it must be given sufficiently in advance of the trial to allow adequate time to prepare a defence. The accused should generally be able to choose his or her own counsel, because of the special role of trust and confidence between the lawyer and the client.[130] However, the accused does not have an unrestricted right to choose assigned counsel, especially if the State is paying the costs.

B.   Right to legal assistance

If accused individuals do not have a lawyer of their choice to represent them, they may have counsel assigned. Under article 14, paragraph 3 (d), of the International Covenant on Civil and Political Rights, the right to have counsel assigned is conditional upon a conclusion by the court that the interests of justice require it. The determination of whether the interests of justice require appointment of counsel is based primarily on the seriousness of the offence, the issues at stake, including the potential sentence and the complexity of the issues. Additionally, the State is required to provide counsel free of charge to the accused if two conditions are met:[131] if the interests of justice require that counsel be appointed and if the accused does not have sufficient funds to pay for a lawyer.

---

[128]See for example, the case of *Foucher v. France*, judgement of the European Court of Human Rights of 18 March 1997.

[129]See Basic Principles on the Role of Lawyers, principle 5; statute of the International Tribunal for the Prosecution of Persons Responsible for Serious Violations of International Humanitarian Law Committed in the Territory of the Former Yugoslavia since 1991, article 21, paragraph 4 (d); Rome Statute of the International Criminal Court (United Nations, *Treaty Series*, vol. 2187, No. 38544), article 55, paragraph 2 (c). See also the International Covenant on Civil and Political Rights, article 14, paragraph 3 (d).

[130]See the International Covenant on Civil and Political Rights, article 14, paragraph 3 (d); Basic Principles on the Role of Lawyers, principle 1.

[131]International Covenant on Civil and Political Rights, article 14, paragraph 3 (d).

C. Exceptional measures

Access to a lawyer is as important for the right to fair trial as it is for the right to liberty. Prompt access to a lawyer is central to the administration of justice and the effective prosecution of offenders. As such, it is an essential element of fair trial guarantees. In the absence of access to a lawyer, the right to fair trial may be meaningless. Effective access to a lawyer means access must be confidential. For example, failure to guarantee confidentiality may make a detainee feel intimidated and not disclose ill-treatment. Nevertheless, effective counter-terrorism practices may sometimes justify certain restrictions to the right of defence, in particular with regard to the arrangements for access to and contacts with counsel, arrangements for the counsel's access to the case file and the use of anonymous testimony.

Such restrictions to the right of defence must be strictly proportionate to their purpose, and compensatory measures to protect the interests of the accused must be taken in order to maintain the fairness of the proceedings and ensure that procedural rights are not drained of their substance.[132]

The right of detained or imprisoned persons to communicate with their legal counsel is a very important one; it is a fundamental right that relates directly to the right of defence.[133]

Communication with legal counsel while imprisoned or detained

Principle 18 of the Body of Principles for the Protection of All Persons under Any Form of Detention or Imprisonment states the following:

- A detained or imprisoned person shall be entitled to communicate and consult with his legal counsel.

- A detained or imprisoned person shall be allowed adequate time and facilities for consultation with his legal counsel.

- The right of a detained or imprisoned person to be visited by and to consult and communicate, without delay or censorship and in full confidentiality, with his legal counsel may not be suspended or restricted save in exceptional circumstances, to be specified by law or lawful regulations, when it is considered indispensable by a judicial or other authority in order to maintain security and good order.

- Interviews between a detained or imprisoned person and his legal counsel may be within sight, but not within the hearing, of a law enforcement official.

- Communications between a detained or imprisoned person and his legal counsel mentioned in the present principle shall be inadmissible as evidence against the detained or imprisoned person unless they are connected with a continuing or contemplated crime.

Other special measures are sometimes considered in order to reconcile the right to counsel with the special circumstances created by the need to prevent acts of terrorism. In some cases, it may be advisable to consider establishing a security clearance system for lawyers

---

[132]Guidelines of the Committee of Ministers of the Council of Europe on human rights and the fight against terrorism (A/57/313, annex I).

[133]For example, see European Court of Human Rights, *Erdem v. Germany*, judgement of 5 July 2001.

who will have access to special files or information or to establish in consultation with the defence bar a list of lawyers who have had either the special training, the security clearance or both to make them more effective at exercising their duties and defending certain individuals accused of terrorist acts under difficult and challenging circumstances. Defence lawyers must also have the means to seek and obtain special protection measures for themselves and for witnesses (lay or expert) who are required to mount an effective defence of their client.

VI. Role of the judiciary

The courts play a pivotal role in promoting the rule of law. Thus, it is necessary to protect the independence of the judiciary. The right to a competent, independent and impartial tribunal is articulated in article 10 of the Universal Declaration of Human Rights and article 14 of the International Covenant on Civil and Political Rights, as well as in regional treaties and conventions including the European Convention for the Protection of Human Rights and Fundamental Freedoms[134] (article 6), the American Convention on Human Rights (article 8) and the African Charter on Human and Peoples' Rights[135] (article 7). An independent, impartial, honest and competent judiciary is integral to upholding the rule of law and engendering public confidence.

The Universal Declaration of Human Rights contains the right to a fair and public hearing by an independent and impartial tribunal (article 10) and the right of the accused to be presumed innocent until proved guilty according to law in a public trial at which he has had all the guarantees necessary for his defence (article 11). In addition, the Basic Principles on the Independence of the Judiciary, adopted by the Seventh United Nations Congress on the Prevention of Crime and the Treatment of Offenders, envisage judges with full authority to act, free from pressures and threats, adequately paid and equipped to carry out their duties.[136] Although that set of standards does not carry the force of law, it provides a model for lawmakers everywhere, who are encouraged to write them into their national constitutions and to enact them into law.

The Basic Principles on the Independence of the Judiciary cover freedom of expression and association; the qualifications, selection and training of judges; conditions of service and tenure; and discipline, suspension and removal of judges. Many countries have formally adopted the Basic Principles and report regularly to the United Nations on their progress and problems, sometimes seeking help with legal education or the monitoring of procedures.[137]

The present chapter examines more closely the question of the independence, impartiality and integrity of the judiciary and its significance from the point of view of ensuring the rights of the accused to a fair trial. It also touches on the procedural guarantees that must be upheld by courts, as well as the question of the security of the courts.

---

[134]United Nations, *Treaty Series*, vol. 213, No. 2889.

[135]United Nations, *Treaty Series*, vol. 1520, No. 26363.

[136]Basic Principles on the Independence of the Judiciary (*Seventh United Nations Congress on the Prevention of Crime and the Treatment of Offenders, Milan, 26 August-6 September 1985: report prepared by the Secretariat* (United Nations publication, Sales No. E.86.IV.1), chap. I, sect. D.2, annex).

[137]See the procedures for the effective implementation of the Basic Principles on the Independence of the Judiciary (Economic and Social Council resolution 1989/60, annex); see also the Bangalore Principles of Judicial Conduct (E/CN.4/2003/65, annex, available at www.unodc.org/pdf/crime/corruption/judicial_group/Bangalore_principles.pdf; United Nations Office on Drugs and Crime, *Commentary on the Bangalore Principles of Judicial Conduct* (2007), available at www.unodc.org/documents/corruption/publications_unodc_commentary-e.pdf.

A.   Independence, impartiality and integrity of the judiciary

The authority granted to the judiciary by a State's constitution and any other enabling statutes are critical in determining the role of the judiciary and the nature of its relationship with the various branches of Government. The source of authority for the administration of justice is found not only in statutes, including the criminal law and criminal procedures codes, but also in rules that are promulgated, often by the courts themselves, with input from representatives of other stakeholders in the criminal justice system. In the absence of such authority, the judiciary may define its authority in rulings and opinions, such a situation tends to be the exception. Those are the primary sources of the legal basis for frameworks and organizations that regulate the behaviour and conduct of judges (e.g. a judicial council).

A close analysis is required to determine whether the existing legal framework supports the independence and integrity of the judiciary or inappropriately impinges on those key values by granting supervisory authority over the judiciary to another branch of Government. That debate often arises in relation to emergency courts and military tribunals.

The Basic Principles on the Independence of the Judiciary set out the elements of the independence of the judiciary in its principles 1-7. As a basic condition, the independence of the judiciary must be guaranteed by the State and enshrined in the constitution or State law.

In order to secure the independence of the judiciary, judicial appointments should be made on the basis of clearly defined criteria and through a public process ensuring that appointments are made based on merit and that there is equality of opportunity for all those who are eligible for judicial office. Arrangements for appropriate security of tenure and protection of levels of remuneration must also be in place, and adequate resources must be available for the judicial system to operate effectively and without any undue restraints.

The judiciary must decide matters impartially, on the basis of facts and the application of law, without any restrictions, improper influences, inducements, pressures, threats or interferences. The courts themselves have exclusive authority to decide whether they have jurisdiction over a matter. There must be no unwarranted interference with the judicial process, including the assignment of judges, by the legislative and executive branches of government.

The Government may not displace the jurisdiction of the ordinary courts through the creation of a tribunal that does not follow established legal procedures. Accused persons have the right to be tried by ordinary courts or tribunals using established legal procedures. Alternative processes such as truth commissions and special tribunals may be established. However, such entities cannot be ad hoc. They must be duly established by law and must afford the minimum guarantees established by international law. The judiciary has the authority and the obligation to ensure that judicial proceedings are conducted fairly and that the rights of all parties are respected.

Independence of the judiciary

"1. The independence of the judiciary shall be guaranteed by the State and enshrined in the Constitution or the law of the country. It is the duty of all governmental and other institutions to respect and observe the independence of the judiciary.

"2. The judiciary shall decide matters before them impartially, on the basis of facts and in accordance with the law, without any restrictions, improper influences, inducements, pressures, threats or interferences, direct or indirect, from any quarter or for any reason.

"3. The judiciary shall have jurisdiction over all issues of a judicial nature and shall have exclusive authority to decide whether an issue submitted for its decision is within its competence as defined by law.

"4. There shall not be any inappropriate or unwarranted interference with the judicial process, nor shall judicial decisions by the courts be subject to revision. This principle is without prejudice to judicial review or to mitigation or commutation by competent authorities of sentences imposed by the judiciary, in accordance with the law.

"5. Everyone shall have the right to be tried by ordinary courts or tribunals using established legal procedures. Tribunals that do not use the duly established procedures of the legal process shall not be created to displace the jurisdiction belonging to the ordinary courts or judicial tribunals.

"6. The principle of the independence of the judiciary entitles and requires the judiciary to ensure that judicial proceedings are conducted fairly and that the rights of the parties are respected.

"7. It is the duty of each Member State to provide adequate resources to enable the judiciary to properly perform its functions."

Basic Principles on the Independence of the Judiciary, articles 1-7.

B. Independence and impartiality of tribunals

The right to trial by an independent and impartial tribunal is central to the due process of law: the Human Rights Committee has stated that it is an absolute right that may suffer no exception.[138] Article 10 of the Universal Declaration of Human Rights affirms the right to a fair trial by an independent and impartial tribunal. Similarly, the International Covenant on Civil and Political Rights, in its article 14, paragraph 1, states the following:

> All persons shall be equal before the courts and tribunals. In the determination of any criminal charge against him, or of his rights and obligations in a suit at law, everyone shall be entitled to a fair and public hearing by a competent, independent and impartial tribunal established by law. The press and the public may be excluded from all or part of a trial for reasons of morals, public order (ordre public) or national security in a democratic society, or when the interest of the private lives of the parties so requires, or to the extent strictly necessary in the opinion of the court in special circumstances where publicity would prejudice the interests of justice; but any judgement rendered in a criminal case or in a suit at law shall be made public except where the interest of juvenile persons otherwise requires or the proceedings concern matrimonial disputes or the guardianship of children.

Article 14, paragraph 2, of the International Covenant states that everyone charged with a criminal offence shall have the right to be presumed innocent until proved guilty according to law.

---

[138]Human Rights Committee, *González del Río v. Peru*, Human Rights Committee Communication No. 263/1987 (CCPR/C/46/D/263/1987), para. 5.2.

In recent years in the context of counter-terrorism measures, United Nations human rights mechanisms have reflected deep concern over the use of military and other special tribunals. The mechanisms underscore that, even under states of emergency, the right to fair trial must be respected. The Special Rapporteur on the independence of judges and lawyers has sent urgent appeals and issued statements in several cases involving allegations of terrorism.[139] The Special Rapporteur and the Working Group on Arbitrary Detention have expressed concerns over the use of military courts and special military commissions to try non-citizens suspected of having links with a terrorist organization, including with respect to the issues of observance by such mechanisms of the principle of equality before the law, fair trial procedures, the selection of those who sit on such commission and courts and appeal procedures contrary to the principle of judicial independence.[140]

In its general comment No. 13, on administration of justice, the Human Rights Committee stated that the use of military courts to try civilians could present serious problems in relation to the provision of fair trials: "Quite often the reason for the establishment of such courts is to enable exceptional procedures to be applied which do not comply with normal standards of justice … The trying of civilians by such courts should be very exceptional and take place under conditions which genuinely afford the full guarantees stipulated in article 14 [of the International Covenant on Civil and Political Rights].[141]

The Human Rights Committee has held that the basic fair trial requirements of article 14 of the International Covenant apply equally to military tribunals and ordinary tribunals. Of particular importance, those tribunals must satisfy the obligations of independence and impartiality. The Committee, noting the existence in certain countries of military tribunals that try civilians, has pointed out that the trying of civilians by such courts should be very exceptional and take place under conditions which genuinely afford the full guarantees stipulated in article 14.

Designation of judges or courts with special jurisdictions

It is sometimes argued that it is necessary to establish courts with special jurisdictions, especially to hear terrorist cases. Although that can be a problematic course of action, national criminal procedures may allow some adaptations without going as far as establishing special courts. In many countries, regular courts have sometimes been given a special jurisdiction or mandate greatly shaped by the nature of the crimes to be prosecuted. For example, it is possible to allow for the centralization of certain cases by identifying a pool of magistrates who will be habilitated to hear certain types of cases and therefore may develop a particular competence, including cases involving terrorist offences. Prosecutions of certain types of cases involving terrorist groups can be centralized in a certain part of the country, allowing a group of judges (as well as prosecutors and defence counsels) to specialize in those cases. The centralization of cases and the specialization of certain magistrates can also make it easier to prevent various attempts at obstructing justice and to protect those involved against possible intimidation or retaliation.

---

[139]E/CN.4/2004/60/Add.1.

[140]E/CN.4/2004/3.

[141]Human Rights Committee, General Comment No. 13 on equality before the courts and the right to a fair and public hearing by an independent court established by law (art. 14), available at http://www2.ohchr.org/english/bodies/hrc/comments.htm.

C. Security of the courts

There have been numerous cases in which terrorists have sought to obstruct justice by threatening prosecutors, judges and other officers of the court or by intimidating or attacking jurors and witnesses. Without proper protection for judges and court personnel, courts are often unable to function effectively or fairly when they are the object of threats or potential threats by terrorist groups or their supporters. Similarly, the criminal justice process can be paralysed by the system's inability to protect all participants against intimidation and retaliation. Part of the core capacity of the criminal justice system to deal with acts of terrorism is capacity to effectively ensure the security of judges, prosecutors and other court personnel, as well as the capacity of jurors, witnesses and all others who participate in court proceedings.

VII. Issues and challenges concerning detention

Individuals who are accused of terrorist crimes are often held in prison, sometimes for a long period of time, awaiting the conclusion of an investigation or a trial. They are unlikely to be released on bail pending trial and likely to be segregated from the inmate population. There are often circumstances that dictate that their contacts with the outside world or with suspected accomplices be limited. Nevertheless, all persons deprived of their liberty in relation to terrorist activities must in all circumstances be treated with due respect for their human dignity and human rights.

"All persons deprived of their liberty shall be treated with humanity and with respect for the inherent dignity of the human person."

International Covenant on Civil and Political Rights, article 10.

Numerous international standards have been developed to ensure that the human rights of prisoners are protected and that their treatment has the priority aim of ensuring their social reintegration. Those standards include the Standard Minimum Rules for the Treatment of Prisoners, the Body of Principles for the Protection of All Persons under Any Form of Detention or Imprisonment, the United Nations Standard Minimum Rules for the Administration of Juvenile Justice (Beijing Rules),[142] the United Nations Rules for the Protection of Juveniles Deprived of Their Liberty,[143] and the Code of Conduct for Law Enforcement Officials,[144] among many other international and regional documents.

Counter-terrorism strategies may require some adjustments to normal prison practices, as long as those modifications are lawful and their application is subject to judicial review. For example, guideline XI of the Council of Europe Guidelines on Human Rights and the Fight against Terrorism, states the following:

"The imperatives of the fight against terrorism may nevertheless require that a person deprived of his/her liberty for terrorist activities be submitted to more severe restrictions than those applied to other prisoners, in particular with regard to:

"(i)   The regulations concerning communications and surveillance of correspondence, including that between counsel and his/her client;

"(ii)   Placing persons deprived of their liberty for terrorist activities in specially secured quarters;

"(iii)   The separation of such persons within a prison or among different prisons, on condition that the measure taken is proportionate to the aim to be achieved."

---

[142]General Assembly resolution 40/33, annex.

[143]General Assembly resolution 45/113, annex.

[144]General Assembly resolution 34/169, annex.

A.   Detention prior to adjudication or during investigation

The Standard Minimum Rules for the Treatment of Prisoners devote a section to prisoners under arrest or awaiting trial (rules 84-93). Those provisions serving as guidelines for prison authorities govern the conditions of detention of pretrial prisoners, the privileges to which they are entitled and access to legal advice and assistance.

In all prisons, those on remand should be treated as a privileged category of prisoners and be able to dress in their own clothes, receive food from the outside, have access to their own doctors, procure reading and writing materials and receive regular visits from their legal advisers as well as assistance in preparing for their trials.

Pretrial detention should be a measure of last resort implemented only to protect society or ensure that a serious offender attends trial at a future date. Time spent on remand should be kept to a minimum and should be applied against any sentence that may eventually be imposed.

Article 10 of the International Covenant on Civil and Political Rights makes it clear that accused persons should be held separately from convicted offenders and be subject to separate treatment appropriate to their status as unconvicted persons.

Individuals who are captured during military operations and are accused of a terrorism-related offence must be dealt with in accordance with the Third and Fourth Geneva Conventions, which contain rules to regulate the detention regime.[145] The Third Geneva Convention contains a comprehensive set of rules determining the treatment and material conditions of detention of members of armed forces taken prisoner. The protection those rules afford prisoners of war is sometimes denied to so-called "illegal combatants" by denying their status as prisoners of war. That can weaken the best-known and strongest pillar of the international humanitarian system.[146] If illegal combatants are treated as civilians, they must be treated in accordance with the Fourth Geneva Convention on the protection, in wartime, of civilian persons. The Convention does not grant any immunity to civilians who have committed serious crimes and does not prevent them from being put on trial, as long as it is a fair trial.

Access to legal counsel

A detained person must be entitled to have the assistance of a legal counsel. According to the Body of Principles for the Protection of All Persons under Any Form of Detention or Imprisonment, the detained person must be promptly informed of his or her rights and be provided with reasonable facility for exercising it.

As mentioned above, persons suspected of terrorist activities who are detained pending trial are entitled to regular reviews of the lawfulness of their detention by a court, and access to legal counsel can help them enforce that right.

---

[145]See the discussion of international humanitarian law in Chapter 3 of this *Handbook*.

[146]Hans-Peter Gasser, "Acts of terror, 'terrorism' and international humanitarian law", *International Review of the Red Cross*, vol. 84, No. 847 (2002), p. 568.

B.   Conditions of detention and custody

As noted above, the International Covenant on Civil and Political Rights affirms that all persons deprived of their liberty shall be treated with humanity and with respect for the inherent dignity of the human person.[147] In order for prison systems to be managed in a humane manner, national policies and legislation concerning prison conditions must be guided by the numerous international standards developed to ensure that the rights of prisoners are protected. Those standards include the Standard Minimum Rules for the Treatment of Prisoners and the Body of Principles for the Protection of All Persons under Any Form of Detention or Imprisonment.

C.   Cruel or inhuman treatment or punishment

Article 1 of the Convention against Torture and Other Cruel, Inhuman or Degrading Treatment or Punishment sets out an internationally agreed definition of acts that constitute torture:

> [T]he term "torture" means any act by which severe pain or suffering, whether physical or mental, is intentionally inflicted on a person for such purposes as obtaining from him or a third person information or a confession, punishing him for an act he or a third person has committed or is suspected of having committed, or intimidating or coercing him or a third person, or for any reason based on discrimination of any kind, when such pain or suffering is inflicted by or at the instigation of or with the consent or acquiescence of a public official or other person acting in an official capacity. It does not include pain or suffering arising only from, inherent in or incidental to lawful sanctions.

"No one shall be subjected to torture or to cruel, inhuman or degrading treatment or punishment."

International Covenant on Civil and Political Rights, article 7.

The essential elements of what constitutes torture as defined in article 1 of the Convention against Torture are the infliction of severe mental or physical pain or suffering, by, or with the consent or acquiescence of, State authorities, for a specific purpose such as gaining information, punishment or intimidation.

Cruel, inhuman or degrading treatment or punishment are also legal terms, referring to ill-treatment that is not necessarily inflicted for a specific purpose but which is conducted with the intent of exposing individuals to conditions that amount to or result in ill-treatment. Exposing a person to conditions reasonably believed to constitute ill-treatment entail responsibility for inflicting that ill-treatment. Degrading treatment may involve pain or suffering that is less severe than that inflicted in the course of torture or cruel or inhuman treatment and usually involves humiliation and debasement of the victim. The essential elements that constitute ill-treatment not amounting to torture are thus reduced to intentional exposure to significant mental or physical pain or suffering, by or with the consent or acquiescence of the State authorities.

Article 11 of the Convention against Torture and Other Cruel, Inhuman or Degrading Treatment or Punishment provides that each State party shall keep under systematic review interrogation rules, instructions, methods and practices as well as arrangements for the

---

[147]International Covenant on Civil and Political Rights, article 10, paragraph 1.

custody and treatment of persons subjected to any form of arrest, detention or imprison-ment in any territory under its jurisdiction, with a view to preventing any cases of torture.

Article 12 of the Convention requires a State party to ensure that its competent authori-ties proceed to a prompt and impartial investigation, wherever there is reasonable ground to believe that an act of torture has been committed in any territory under its jurisdiction.

Article 13 of the Convention requires a State party to ensure that any individual who alleges he has been subjected to torture in any territory under its jurisdiction has the right to complain to, and to have his case promptly and impartially examined by, its competent authorities. Steps shall be taken to ensure that the complainant and witnesses are protected against all ill-treatment or intimidation as a consequence of his complaint or any evidence given.

In terms of protecting a person's legal rights and safeguarding him/her against ill-treatment and torture, there are a number of fundamental safeguards that should apply from the outset of a person's detention:

- The right to inform a close relative or someone else of the detained person's choice of his/her situation immediately[148]

- The right to immediate access to a lawyer[149]

- The right to a medical examination and the right of access to a doctor, ideally of the detainee's own choice, at all times, in addition to any official medical examination[150]

- The right to be brought "promptly" before a judge for a determination of the legality of the detention and whether it may continue[151]

- The right to be informed immediately about the reasons for arrest and rights under the law, in a language they understand[152]

---

[148]Standard Minimum Rules for the Treatment of Prisoners, rule 92; Body of Principles for the Protection of All Persons under Any Form of Detention or Imprisonment, principle 16.

[149]Body of Principles for the Protection of All Persons under Any Form of Detention or Imprisonment, principle 17.

[150]Standard Minimum Rules for the Treatment of Prisoners, rule 91; Body of Principles for the Protection of All Persons under Any Form of Detention or Imprisonment, principle 24; European Committee for the Prevention of Torture and Inhuman or Degrading Treatment or Punishment, *2nd General Report on the CPT's activities*, covering the period 1 January to 31 December 1991 (Strasbourg, Council of Europe, 1992), available at www.cpt.coe.int/en/annual/rep-02.htm; Council of Europe, Recommendation Rec(2001)10 of the Committee of Ministers to member States on the European Code of Police Ethics, article 57.

[151]Body of Principles for the Protection of All Persons under Any Form of Detention or Imprisonment, principle 11. While there is no precise definition for "promptly", more than 72 hours is often considered excessive and is the maximum established by the model code of criminal procedure (draft, 30 May 2006), article 125 bis.

[152]Body of Principles for the Protection of All Persons under Any Form of Detention or Imprisonment, principles 10, 13 and 14.

Other relevant international standards

In addition to international human rights law and the laws of armed conflict, a considerable range of other rules and standards have been developed to safeguard the right of all people to protection against torture and other forms of ill-treatment. Although not of themselves legally binding, they represent agreed principles that should be adhered to by all States and can provide important guidance for judges and prosecutors. Those standards include the following:

- Standard Minimum Rules for the Treatment of Prisoners (1957, amended in 1977)

- Declaration on the Protection of All Persons from Being Subjected to Torture and Other Cruel, Inhuman or Degrading Treatment or Punishment (1975)

- Code of Conduct for Law Enforcement Officials (1979)

- Principles of Medical Ethics relevant to the role of health personnel, particularly physicians, in the protection of prisoners and detainees against torture and other cruel, inhuman or degrading treatment or punishment (1982)

- Declaration of Basic Principles of Justice for Victims of Crime and Abuse of Power (1985)

- Basic Principles on the Independence of the Judiciary (1985)

- United Nations Standard Minimum Rules for the Administration of Juvenile Justice (the Beijing Rules) (1985)

- Body of Principles for the Protection of All Persons under Any Form of Detention or Imprisonment (1988)

- Principles on the Effective Prevention and Investigation of Extra-legal, Arbitrary and Summary Executions (1989)

- Basic Principles for the Treatment of Prisoners (1990)

- Basic Principles on the Role of Lawyers (1990)

- Guidelines on the Role of Prosecutors (1990)

- United Nations Rules for the Protection of Juveniles Deprived of their Liberty (1990)

- Basic Principles on the Use of Force and Firearms by Law Enforcement Officials (1990)

- Principles for the Protection of Persons with Mental Illness and the Improvement of Mental Health Care (1991)

- Declaration on the Protection of All Persons from Enforced Disappearance (1992)

- Principles on the Effective Investigation and Documentation of Torture and Other Cruel, Inhuman or Degrading Treatment or Punishment (Istanbul Protocol) (1999)

Investigation of torture
Istanbul Protocol

The Commission on Human Rights, in its resolution 2000/43, and the General Assembly, in its resolution 55/89, drew the attention of Governments to the Principles on the Effective Investigation and Documentation of Torture and Other Cruel, Inhuman or Degrading Treatment or Punishment (Istanbul Protocol) and strongly encouraged Governments to reflect upon the Principles as a useful tool in combating torture.

"1. The purposes of effective investigation and documentation of torture and other cruel, inhuman or degrading treatment or punishment (hereafter "torture or other ill-treatment") include the following:

"*(a)* Clarification of the facts and establishment and acknowledgment of individual and State responsibility for victims and their families;

"*(b)* Identification of measures needed to prevent recurrence;

"*(c)* Facilitation of prosecution and/or, as appropriate, disciplinary sanctions for those indicated by the investigation as being responsible and demonstration of the need for full reparation and redress from the State, including fair and adequate financial compensation and provision of the means for medical care and rehabilitation.

"2.   States shall ensure that complaints and reports of torture or ill treatment are promptly and effectively investigated. Even in the absence of an express complaint, an investigation should be undertaken if there are other indications that torture or ill-treatment might have occurred. The investigators, who shall be independent of the suspected perpetrators and the agency they serve, shall be competent and impartial. They shall have access to, or be empowered to commission investigations by, impartial medical or other experts. The methods used to carry out such investigations shall meet the highest professional standards and the findings shall be made public.

"3.   *(a)*   The investigative authority shall have the power and obligation to obtain all the information necessary to the inquiry. The persons conducting the investigation shall have at their disposal all the necessary budgetary and technical resources for effective investigation. They shall also have the authority to oblige all those acting in an official capacity allegedly involved in torture or ill-treatment to appear and testify. The same shall apply to any witness. To this end, the investigative authority shall be entitled to issue summonses to witnesses, including any officials allegedly involved, and to demand the production of evidence.

"*(b)* Alleged victims of torture or ill-treatment, witnesses, those conducting the investigation and their families shall be protected from violence, threats of violence or any other form of intimidation that may arise pursuant to the investigation. Those potentially implicated in torture or ill-treatment shall be removed from any position of control or power, whether direct or indirect, over complainants, witnesses and their families, as well as those conducting the investigation.

"4.   Alleged victims of torture or ill-treatment and their legal representatives shall be informed of, and have access to, any hearing, as well as to all information relevant to the investigation, and shall be entitled to present other evidence.

"5.   *(a)*   In cases in which the established investigative procedures are inadequate because of insufficient expertise or suspected bias, or because of the apparent existence of a pattern of abuse, or for other substantial reasons, States shall ensure that investigations are undertaken through an independent commission of inquiry or similar procedure. Members of such a commission shall be chosen for their recognized impartiality, competence and independence as individuals. In particular, they shall be independent of any suspected perpetrators and the institutions or agencies they may serve. The commission shall have the authority to obtain all information necessary to the inquiry and shall conduct the inquiry as provided for under these Principles. Under certain circumstances, professional ethics may require information to be kept confidential. These requirements should be respected.

"*(b)*   A written report, made within a reasonable time, shall include the scope of the inquiry, procedures and methods used to evaluate evidence as well as conclusions and recommendations based on findings of fact and on applicable law. Upon completion, the report shall be made public. It shall also describe in detail specific events that were found to have occurred and the evidence upon which such findings were based and list the names of witnesses who testified, with the exception of those whose identities have been withheld for their own protection. The State shall, within a reasonable period of time, reply to the report of the investigation and, as appropriate, indicate steps to be taken in response.

"6.   *(a)*   Medical experts involved in the investigation of torture or ill treatment shall behave at all times in conformity with the highest ethical standards and, in particular, shall obtain informed consent before any examination is undertaken. The examination must conform to established standards of medical practice. In particular, examinations shall be conducted in private under the control of the medical expert and outside the presence of security agents and other government officials.

"*(b)* The medical expert should promptly prepare an accurate written report."

General Assembly resolution 55/89, annex, paras. 1-6.

D.   Security and safety of prisoners

"Security" of prisoners refers to the obligation of the prison service to prevent prisoners from escaping. Conventional means of security include walls, bars, locks, keys, gates, movement detectors, other technological devices and perimeter sterile areas. The "safety" of prisoners refers to the requirement to maintain good order and control in prison to prevent prisoners being disruptive and to protect the vulnerable. Safety measures in prisons should be supported by a disciplinary system that is fair and just. Security and safety procedures include proper categorization and assessment, searching and standing operating procedures.

The situation of people suspected of terrorism may be very different from that of other inmates. Exceptional security measures may often be justified. The proper classification of prisoners based on risk assessment is one of the most important steps prison managers must take to ensure safety and security in their prisons. The security measures to which prisoners are subject should be the minimum necessary to achieve their secure custody.

Detainees and prisoners who are held in relation to terrorist activities or conspiracies may need special protection measures to ensure their safety. That often involves various forms of segregation or solitary detention.

Security and safety of witnesses and informants in prison

Some special safety and protection measures are necessary when a witness or an informant is being detained. Witnesses who are incarcerated can be particularly vulnerable, and their protection poses some distinct challenges to the authorities,[153] the most common relating to the presence of other inmates who want to prevent them from testifying or who may themselves intimidate or harm the witnesses. Co-mingling of protected witnesses with the general inmate population is generally inadvisable because it creates opportunities for violence, threats and intimidation. Co-mingling occurs not only during incarceration but also during transportation to court or in the court lock-ups.

Witness safety issues relating to communication with the outside world (such as by telephone or letters) and visits must be examined carefully. Weaknesses in information management systems, at either the institution or the court level, can significantly add to the risks faced by the protected witness. Dangerous mistakes can also occur because of poor communication between prison authorities and professionals from other agencies who share a responsibility for the protection of the witnesses.

Intimidation of protected witnesses who are detained can be very hard to detect, particularly indirect intimidation. There is often a need to take measures to protect the families of custodial witnesses.[154] In some instances, the corruption or the intimidation of prison personnel can introduce a major element of risk for the witnesses who are being detained. It is therefore often necessary to limit the circle of individual staff members who have access to the protected inmates and to information about them. In some instances, detained witnesses may be transferred to another province, state or country for their protection, provided that the necessary agreements between the jurisdictions exist.

[153]S. Cooley, *Jailhouse Witness Protection Task Force: Final Report* (Los Angeles, District Attorney's Office, 2004).

[154]Australia, Parliamentary Joint Committee on the National Crime Authority, Witness Protection (Canberra, Australian Government Publishing Service, 1988), p. xii.

In some jurisdictions, correctional authorities have established a special "witness protection unit" with special security measures and better quality accommodation for inmates. It is also possible to have alternative housing and transportation options for endangered witnesses. It is often recognized that because protected witnesses must serve their sentence in harsher circumstances than would otherwise be the case, their situation should receive special consideration at the time of making parole or release decisions. Sometimes, special arrangements concerning their supervision on probation or parole must be made. Protected witnesses serving a prison sentence must be given clear assurance as to the arrangements proposed for their protection upon release.

E. Transfer of detainees and prisoners

The international community has addressed in various contexts the questions of the transfer of prisoners and the treatment of foreign prisoners. In 1985, the Seventh United Nations Congress on the Prevention of Crime and the Treatment of Offenders adopted the Model Agreement on the Transfer of Foreign Prisoners and recommendations on the treatment of foreign prisoners.[155] In the context of the fight against terrorism, the question of the transfer of prisoners, as a means to support the investigation and prosecution of terrorist crimes, is also addressed.

The International Convention for the Suppression of Terrorist Bombings[156] and the International Convention for the Suppression of the Financing of Terrorism deal with the transfer of persons who are being detained or serving sentences. Thus, "[a] person who is being detained or is serving a sentence in the territory of one State party whose presence in another State party is requested for purposes of identification, testimony or otherwise providing assistance in obtaining evidence for the investigation or prosecution of offences set forth in [the relevant articles of the two Conventions] may be transferred",[157] provided that the following conditions are met: the person must freely give his or her informed consent and the competent authorities of both States must agree to that transfer, subject to such conditions as those States deem appropriate.

For the purposes of this procedure, the State to which the transfer is made has the authority and obligation to keep the person concerned in custody unless otherwise requested or authorized by the State from which the person was transferred. It must also discharge without delay its obligation to return the person to the custody of the State from which the person was transferred as agreed beforehand or as otherwise agreed by the competent authorities of both States. Furthermore, it may not require the State from which the person was transferred to initiate extradition proceedings for the return of the person.

Various guarantees are provided. The person transferred has to receive credit for service of the sentence being served in the State from which he or she was transferred for time spent in the custody of the State to which he or she was transferred. Unless the State from which a person is to be transferred so agrees, that person, whatever his or her

---

[155]Model Agreement on the Transfer of Foreign Prisoners and recommendations on the treatment of foreign prisoners (*Seventh United Nations Congress on the Prevention of Crime and the Treatment of Offenders, Milan, 26 August-6 September 1985: report prepared by the Secretariat* (United Nations publication, Sales No. E.86.IV.1), chap. I, sect. D.1, annexes I and II).

[156]United Nations, *Treaty Series*, vol. 2149, No. 37517.

[157]International Convention for the Suppression of Terrorist Bombings, article 13; International Convention for the Suppression of the Financing of Terrorism, article 16.

nationality, may not be prosecuted or detained or subjected to any other restriction of his or her personal liberty in the territory of the State to which that person is transferred in respect of acts or convictions prior to his or her departure from the territory of the State from which he or she was transferred.

The transfer must always be lawful and provide the necessary procedural safeguards to protect the rights of the individuals involved. The obligations of States under article 7 of the International Covenant on Civil and Political Rights prevents them from expelling, transferring or otherwise removing a prisoner if that may expose him or her to the danger of torture, inhuman or degrading treatment or punishment.

In the context of counter-terrorism, some States have made use of diplomatic assurances, memorandums of understanding and other forms of diplomatic agreement to justify the return or irregular transfer of individuals suspected of terrorist activity to countries where they may face a real risk of torture or other serious human rights abuse.

In its opinion on the international legal obligations of Council of Europe member States in respect of secret detention facilities and inter-State transport of prisoners, the European Commission for Democracy through Law (Venice Commission) emphasized the following:

> "The assessment of the reality of the risk must be carried out very rigorously. The risk assessment will depend upon the circumstances, meaning both the rights which risk being violated and the situation in the receiving State. The diplomatic assurances which are usually provided by the requesting State in order to exclude human rights breaches in its territory after the extradition or deportation is carried out may be appropriate as concerns risks of application of the death penalty or for fair trial violations, because such risks can in most instances be monitored satisfactorily. On the other hand, as regards the risk of torture, monitoring is impracticable in the vast majority of conceivable cases, especially bearing in mind the fact that, even after conviction in a criminal case, a State may torture a prisoner for the purpose of obtaining information. At the same time, it is impracticable to have a "life-long" responsibility for people who are removed out of the country."[158]

This situation raises the question of the value of diplomatic assurances. These arrangements do not, by themselves, provide sufficient protection against torture or other serious human rights abuses. However, as was pointed by the Venice Commission, the acceptance of such assurances is in principle the expression of the necessary good faith and mutual trust between friendly States. Nevertheless, for the assurances to be sufficient to fulfil the duty of a State, the terms need to be unequivocal and reflect the scope of the obligation by which the issuing State is legally bound.

F. Preventive detention

In recent years, there have been numerous reports, in the context of counter-terrorism measures, of situations in which individuals were detained for a long period of time without ever being charged for a specific offence, without access to counsel, access to courts or information on the reasons for their arrest and detention. The Human Rights Committee

---

[158]Council of Europe, European Commission for Democracy through Law (Venice Commission), Opinion on the international legal obligations of Council of Europe member States in respect of secret detention facilities and inter-State transport of prisoners, adopted at the 66th plenary session, Venice, 17-18 March 2006.

has severely criticized those practices. The Committee issued a general comment on the lawfulness of preventive detention in 1982: "If so-called preventive detention is used, for reasons of public security, it must be controlled by these same provisions, i.e. it must not be arbitrary, and must be based on grounds and procedures established by law, information of the reasons must be given and court control of the detention must be available as well as compensation in the case of a breach".[159]

Most forms of preventive detention and administrative detention without a judicial order are contrary to fundamental human rights.[160]

Administrative and preventive detention often lack the safeguards that are integral to the criminal justice system. For administrative detention to comply with human rights principles, it must be executed on such grounds and in accordance with such procedures as are established by law.

Arbitrary detention is never justifiable. The Working Group on Arbitrary Detention, in its reports to the Commission on Human Rights, expressed grave concerns about several instances in arbitrary detention where detainees had no right or means to challenge their unlawful detention. The Commission, in turn, reaffirmed that no justification can be used in any circumstances, whether conflict, war or state of exception, to abrogate the right to challenge unlawful detention.

The Working Group on Arbitrary Detention found the following:

> The use of "administrative detention" under public security legislation, migration laws or other related administrative law, resulting in a deprivation of liberty for unlimited time or for very long periods without effective judicial oversight, as a means to detain persons suspected of involvement in terrorism or other crimes, is not compatible with international human rights law. The Working Group therefore recommends that all States review their legislation and practice so as to ensure that persons suspected of criminal activity or any other activities giving rise under domestic law to deprivation of liberty are in fact afforded the guarantees applicable to criminal proceedings.[161]

G. Complaint procedures

Most prison legislation provides for a set of written procedures that allow prisoners to register any complaints they have regarding their treatment in prison. Prisoners should be given written information about the complaints procedures, prison rules and regulations, as part of an information pack on entry to prison. The procedures should be clearly laid out in a way that can be understood both by prisoners and by the staff who deal directly with the prisoners.

---

[159]Human Rights Committee, General Comment No. 8 on the right to liberty and security of persons (art. 9), para. 4, available at http://www2.ohchr.org/english/bodies/hrc/comments.htm.

[160]Edward J. Flynn, "Counter-terrorism and human rights ...", p. 40. See also Ben Power, "Preventative detention of terrorist suspects: a review of the law in Australia, Canada and the United Kingdom", paper prepared for the 21st International Conference of the International Society for the Reform of Criminal Law, Vancouver, Canada, 22-26 June 2007, p. 2.

[161]E/CN.4/2005/6, para. 77.

Provision of information to prisoners and the handling of their complaints
Standard Minimum Rules for the Treatment of Prisoners

"35. (1) Every prisoner on admission shall be provided with written information about the regulations governing the treatment of prisoners of his category, the disciplinary requirements of the institution, the authorized methods of seeking information and making complaints, and all such other matters as are necessary to enable him to understand both his rights and his obligations and to adapt himself to the life of the institution.

"(2) If a prisoner is illiterate, the aforesaid information shall be conveyed to him orally.

"36. (1) Every prisoner shall have the opportunity each week day of making requests or complaints to the director of the institution or the officer authorized to represent him.

"(2) It shall be possible to make requests or complaints to the inspector of prisons during his inspection. The prisoner shall have the opportunity to talk to the inspector or to any other inspecting officer without the director or other members of the staff being present.

"(3) Every prisoner shall be allowed to make a request or complaint, without censorship as to substance but in proper form, to the central prison administration, the judicial authority or other proper authorities through approved channels.

"(4) Unless it is evidently frivolous or groundless, every request or complaint shall be promptly dealt with and replied to without undue delay."

Standard Minimum Rules for the Treatment of Prisoners, rules 35 and 36.

There must also be a procedure in place by which prisoners can make confidential written complaints to a person or institution independent of the prison administration, such as a prison ombudsman, a judge or magistrate, if they feel that the prison administration is failing to respond to their complaints or if they are lodging a complaint against a disciplinary decision. There must be effective processes in place for hearing appeals, complaints, allegations and grievances against the decisions made by the prison administration.

Principle 33 of the Body of Principles for the Protection of All Persons under Any Form of Detention or Imprisonment states the following:

"1. A detained or imprisoned person or his counsel shall have the right to make a request or complaint regarding his treatment, in particular in case of torture or other cruel, inhuman or degrading treatment, to the authorities responsible for the administration of the place of detention and to higher authorities and, when necessary, to appropriate authorities vested with reviewing or remedial powers.

"2. In those cases where neither the detained or imprisoned person nor his counsel has the possibility to exercise his rights under paragraph 1 of the present principle, a member of the family of the detained or imprisoned person or any other person who has knowledge of the case may exercise such rights.

"3. Confidentiality concerning the request or complaint shall be maintained if so requested by the complainant.

"4. Every request or complaint shall be promptly dealt with and replied to without undue delay. If the request or complaint is rejected or, in case of inordinate delay, the complainant shall be entitled to bring it before a judicial or other authority. Neither the detained or imprisoned person nor any complainant under paragraph 1 of the present principle shall suffer prejudice for making a request or complaint."

VIII. Role of the criminal justice system in protecting the rights of victims of terrorist crimes

States have a duty to provide protection and assistance to victims of crime, including acts of terrorism. This victim-centred approach has become an increasingly important and recognized part of contemporary criminal justice practice. There are a number of ways in which individuals can become victims of terrorist crimes. Terrorist attacks typically target the civilian population and in the process victimize large numbers of individuals. Victimization may take various forms: the death of a large number of civilians, material losses, physical injury and psychological trauma for surviving victims, and long-term damage to quality of life. The criminal justice system has to be able to deal with the various forms of victimization.

Duty of States to provide legal remedy for violations of human rights

Each State Party to the present Covenant undertakes:

(a)   To ensure that any person whose rights or freedoms as herein recognized are violated shall have an effective remedy, notwithstanding that the violation has been committed by persons acting in an official capacity;

(b   To ensure that any person claiming such a remedy shall have his right thereto determined by competent judicial, administrative or legislative authorities, or by any other competent authority provided for by the legal system of the State, and to develop the possibilities of judicial remedy;

(c)   To ensure that the competent authorities shall enforce such remedies when granted.

International Covenant on Civil and Political Rights, article 2, paragraph 3.

Victims' rights have been articulated in a number of international instruments and in many cases incorporated into the national legislation of States. Since 1945, international law has made progress in the recognition of individual rights in this regard. Affirmation of the right to redress of victims of human rights violations became part of the efforts to protect individual human rights. More recent developments, such as the inclusion of victims' rights to reparations and participation in the Statute of the International Criminal Court, highlight the centrality of victims in the criminal justice system and, by extension, the response of that system to terrorism. It is important to emphasize that while victims of terrorist activities were perhaps not foreseen—or at least not expressly mentioned—in human rights instruments—to the extent that terrorism, as an attack on civilians, is an affront to the human rights of the victims, those victims have the rights enumerated in the relevant treaties.

The United Nations Global Counter-Terrorism Strategy directly addresses the issue of victims of terrorist acts. It lists measures to address the conditions conducive to the spread of terrorism, including measures to counter the "dehumanization of victims of terrorism in all its forms and manifestations". The Strategy encourages the creation of national systems of assistance, which would "promote the needs of victims of terrorism and their families and facilitate the normalization of their lives".

A.   Victims in international law

International human rights and humanitarian law establish several duties in relation to victims of human rights violations. Those duties include the following:

- The duty to provide victims with equal and effective access to justice irrespective of who may be the ultimate bearer of responsibility for the violation;
- The duty to afford appropriate remedies to victims;
- The duty to provide for or facilitate reparation to victims.

A State's duty to provide a domestic legal remedy to a victim of violations of human rights and international humanitarian law committed on its territory is well established in international law. The existence of that duty is grounded in several international and regional conventions. With respect to human rights norms, the International Covenant on Civil and Political Rights ensures, in its article 2, paragraph 3, that victims of human rights violations have the right to an effective remedy, including the right to have such a remedy determined by competent judicial, administrative or legislative authorities and to have that remedy enforced when granted.[162]

Numerous international declarations reaffirm the duty of States to provide a remedy for victims of human rights abuses and violations of international humanitarian law.[163] A comprehensive articulation of this duty is found in the Declaration of Basic Principles of Justice for Victims of Crime and Abuse of Power.[164] The Declaration is the most comprehensive instrument on justice for victims. It provides guidance on measures that should be taken at the national, regional and international levels to improve access to justice and fair treatment, restitution, compensation, protection and assistance for victims of crime and abuse of power. In adopting the Declaration, the General Assembly called upon Member States to take the necessary steps to give effect to the provisions of the Declaration. In its resolution 2005/20 of 2005, the Economic and Social Council adopted the Guidelines on Justice in Matters involving Child Victims and Witnesses of Crime.

Also in 2005, the Commission on Human Rights adopted the Basic Principles and Guidelines on the Right to a Remedy and Reparation for Victims of Gross Violations of International Human Rights Law and Serious Violations of International Humanitarian Law.[165] In addition, in April 2005, the Commission on Human Rights took note of the revised Set of Principles for the Protection and Promotion of Human Rights through Action to Combat Impunity.[166] That set of principles includes the right to know, the right to justice, the right to reparation and guarantees of non-recurrence.

The Organized Crime Convention and the Convention against Corruption also contain various provisions concerning victim protection and victim assistance, including international cooperation in protecting and assisting victims.[167]

---

[162]International Covenant on Civil and Political Rights, article 2, paragraph 3.

[163] See, for example, the Universal Declaration of Human Rights, article 8; Declaration on the Protection of All Persons from Being Subjected to Torture and Other Cruel, Inhuman or Degrading Treatment or Punishment (General Assembly resolution 3452 (XXX), annex), article 11.

[164]General Assembly resolution 40/34, annex.

[165]Basic Principles and Guidelines on the Right to a Remedy and Reparation for Victims of Gross Violations of International Human Rights Law and Serious Violations of International Humanitarian Law (General Assembly resolution 60/147, annex), available at http://www2.ohchr.org/english/law/remedy.htm.

[166]E/CN.4/2005/102/Add.1.

[167]United Nations Convention against Transnational Organized Crime, articles 24 and 25; United Nations Convention against Corruption, article 32.

B. Definition of the term "victims"

In paragraph 1 of the Declaration of Basic Principles of Justice for Victims of Crime and Abuse of Power, "victims" is defined as follows: "'Victims' means persons who, individually or collectively, have suffered harm, including physical or mental injury, emotional suffering, economic loss or substantial impairment of their fundamental rights, through acts or omissions that are in violation of criminal laws operative within Member States, including those proscribing criminal abuse of power."

That definition essentially captures all situations where people are victimized as a result of the crimes committed by terrorist organizations. When the victimization is the result of violations of human rights law or international humanitarian law or refugee law, the definition provided in paragraph 8 of the Basic Principles and Guidelines on the Right to a Remedy and Reparation for Victims of Gross Violations of International Human Rights Law and International Humanitarian Law is also relevant:

> [V]ictims are persons who individually or collectively suffered harm, including physical or mental injury, emotional suffering, economic loss or substantial impairment of their fundamental rights, through acts or omissions that constitute gross violations of international human rights law, or serious violations of international humanitarian law. Where appropriate, and in accordance with domestic law, the term "victim" also includes the immediate family or dependants of the direct victim and persons who have suffered harm in intervening to assist victims in distress or to prevent victimization.

C. Responding to the needs of victims of terrorism

Victims of terrorist crimes must be treated with compassion and respect for their dignity. They are entitled to access to the mechanisms of justice and to prompt redress, as provided for by national legislation, for the harm that they have suffered. Judicial and administrative mechanisms should be established and strengthened where necessary to enable victims to obtain redress through formal or informal procedures that are expeditious, fair, inexpensive and accessible.

To respond to the needs of victims of terrorist crimes, measures should be in place to provide the following:

- Inform victims of their role in the criminal justice process; the nature of the co-operation that is expected from them; and the scope, timing and progress of the criminal proceedings, as well as the outcome of the proceedings;
- Allow the views and concerns of victims to be presented and considered at appropriate stages of the proceedings where their personal interests are affected, without prejudice to the accused and consistent with the relevant procedures of the national criminal justice system;
- Provide proper assistance to victims throughout the judicial proceedings;
- Minimize inconvenience to victims, protect their privacy when necessary, and ensure their safety and that of their families;
- Protect victims from potential intimidation and retaliation;
- Avoid unnecessary delay in the disposition of cases and the execution of orders or decrees granting awards to victims;

- Offer victims the necessary material, medical, psychological and social assistance through governmental, voluntary and community-based means;
- Offer victims access to restitution and compensation.

In many countries, experience has shown that an effective way to address the many needs of crime victims is to establish programmes that provide social, psychological, emotional and financial support and effectively help victims within criminal justice and social institutions. In addition to provisions allowing victims to bring civil claims against perpetrators, some countries have enacted national legislation recognizing victims' rights to compensation and to participation in criminal proceedings. Those possibilities enhance recognition of the suffering of victims. Allowing victim participation in criminal proceedings and recognizing the right of victims to be informed of progress in the case serves to rebalance a criminal justice system that would otherwise heavily favour perpetrators and offenders.

At a practical level, the right of victims to be informed of their rights and of the existence of procedures from which they can benefit is perhaps the most important concern. Those who come into contact with victims in the course of justice—police, social workers, defence attorneys, prosecutors and judges—should be required to brief victims of their rights and direct them to where they can obtain help when they need it.

D. Improving the criminal justice system's response to victims

Criminal justice officials and policymakers can help ensure that criminal justice systems are responsive to the needs of victims and respectful of their rights by doing the following:

- Assessing the needs of victims, in particular victims of terrorism or counter-terrorism measures, and assessing how those needs are addressed;
- Assessing the availability of existing resources to meet victims' needs and the capacity of existing agencies to provide effective protection and assistance to victims of crime;
- Reviewing existing national policies, procedures and laws for dealing with victims of crime, abuse of power and violations of human rights;
- Reviewing how existing practices in every aspect of the criminal justice system are affecting victims of crime and how those practices can be improved;
- Assessing and improving as necessary access by victims to justice and redress and the conditions of that access;
- Assessing and improving as necessary access by victims to legal counsel in seeking redress and access to justice;
- Assessing the various forms of compensation, if any, victims of crime and victims of violations of human rights may have access to and improving existing compensation mechanisms as necessary;
- Assessing specifically how victims of abuse of power are treated and what recourses and access to redress available to them;
- Reviewing and enhancing national legal frameworks, including how they specifically address the rights of victims of abuse of power and victims of violations of human rights;

- Developing national policies for victim assistance and victim protection;
- Developing the capacity of existing institutions and agencies to offer assistance services for victims;
- Providing training for law enforcement and justice officials in human rights and the rights of victims;
- Providing training in the use of testimonial assistance techniques to protect the safety, privacy and identity of victims who testify as witnesses in court;
- Providing training for and supporting assistance workers and professionals working with victims and witnesses;
- Developing court-based and police-based assistance services for victims and witnesses;
- Supporting non-governmental organizations involved in providing assistance and support to victims of crime and victims of violations of human rights;
- Developing the capacity of local authorities to cooperate internationally in the protection of victims, compensation for the harm suffered by victims and the safe repatriation of victims when necessary.

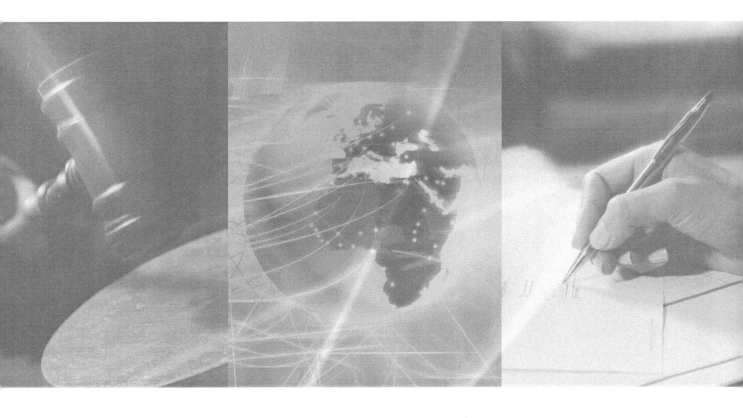

Part three

Criminal justice accountability and oversight mechanisms

I. Oversight of law enforcement

The strength of the criminal justice response to terrorism resides in the fact that it is governed by the rule of law and remains accountable to the society in which it operates. The accountability of the system by means of the media and the political process needs to be reinforced by mechanisms that ensure the system's transparency and are capable of addressing its weaknesses. Part three of the *Handbook* briefly examines the processes that must be in place to ensure the accountability of the various components of the criminal justice system.

Effective counter-terrorism responses rely on effective and credible law enforcement agencies that enjoy the trust and confidence of the population. Civilian oversight of the police in the context of counter-terrorism strategies will ensure greater transparency of those counter-terrorism policies and enhance public trust in them. Ensuring police integrity is fundamental to good governance and is essential in gaining public trust and achieving public safety. Moreover, because the police are often the most visible and most directly encountered part of government, the level of confidence and trust of a nation in its police often reflects the trust and confidence held in its Government.

Standards are less likely to be compromised if they are being monitored. Thus, public confidence and trust in the police can be enhanced and maintained through clear accountability, effective oversight and transparent integrity.

In setting international standards for policing, the General Assembly in its resolution 34/169 of 17 December 1979, adopted the Code of Conduct for Law Enforcement Officials. The Code establishes the following duties for law enforcement officials:

- Fulfil at all times the duty imposed upon them by law, by serving the community and by protecting all persons against illegal acts;

- Respect and protect human dignity and maintain and uphold the human rights of all persons;

- Use force only when strictly necessary and to the extent required for the performance of their duty;

- Keep matters of a confidential nature confidential;

- Not inflict, instigate or tolerate any act of torture or other cruel, inhuman or degrading treatment or punishment;

- Ensure the full protection and health of persons in their custody;

- Abstain from any act of corruption;

- To the best of their capability, prevent and rigorously oppose any violations of the Code.

The Code is supported by the Guidelines for the Effective Implementation of the Code of Conduct for Law Enforcement Officials,[168] which call for the Code to be introduced

---

[168] Economic and Social Council resolution 2002/13, annex.

into national legislation and practice. The Guidelines also emphasize the importance of key drivers in the institutionalization of police integrity, including the selection, education and training of law enforcement officials, their salaries, working conditions, discipline and supervision, and the need for mechanisms for the receipt and processing of complaints by members of the public. The Code and the Guidelines are invaluable in establishing benchmarks for the oversight capacity and integrity of police systems.

The operational independence of the police must be balanced by accountability. In order for the police to continue to enjoy their necessary operational independence, they must actively show that they adhere to policies and legislation that were formulated to guide their actions and are willing and able to account for these actions.[169]

General means of accountability

The police can be held accountable through a number of different and often complementary mechanisms, including the media, political accountability, criminal courts, internal discipline, civil actions, and specialized mechanisms for complaints and oversight.

Accountability can be promoted in the following ways:

- Having in place a sound governance structure and processes for the police, including a legislated framework to guide its operation and police boards or commissions;
- Managing for performance and accountability by establishing internal reporting mechanisms for critical incidents and use of force, on outside activities and employment of offices and on gifts and potential conflicts of interest;
- Ensuring that effective supervisory practices are adhered to;
- Developing performance targets, performance indicators and sound financial reporting practices;
- Having in place a fair and effective disciplinary process;
- Establishing a citizen complaints review mechanism and/or a civilian oversight mechanism (e.g. a police auditor).

Police officers may be held accountable in a number of ways. They may be made accountable for their performance and productivity, for example, by making use of targets or objectives set by government or the local community. But, more important, the police must be held accountable for how they exercise the power entrusted in them. One can distinguish at least four levels of accountability to which the police must be subjected:

- Holding police agencies accountable for the services that they deliver (performance and quality of services);
- Holding police agencies accountable for the resources at their disposal and how they utilize them;

[169]A. Osse, *Understanding Policing: A Resource for Human Rights Activists* (Amsterdam, Amnesty International, 2006), p. 117.

- Holding individual officers accountable for how they conduct themselves, how they treat citizens and whether they respect citizens' rights;

- Holding police managers accountable for how they deal with incidents of officer misconduct.

Disciplinary mechanisms

Police officers can be engaged in various forms of misconduct having varying degree of seriousness and different kinds of consequences. Such misconduct can include criminal behaviour, mistreatment of prisoners or suspects, tampering or fabrication of evidence, inappropriate use of informants, unauthorized disclosure of information, false testimony, acceptance of bribes and various other forms of corruption. Appropriate and fair mechanisms need to be in place to deal with all potential forms of police misconduct.

Civilian oversight mechanisms

Several models can be considered and adapted to different national contexts. The goal is to "maximize in-house police management responsibility while simultaneously guarding against the enormous capacity and systematic tendency of police organizations to protect corrupt colleagues, cover up improper practices and evade accountability".[170] A distinction could perhaps be drawn between civilian review and civilian control models. The civilian control model involves genuinely independent investigation and adjudication. The civilian review model, in which a civilian body reviews the finding of a police investigation, is weaker because of the police capacity to subvert the process.

[170]T. Prenzler and C. Ronken, "Models of police oversight: a critique", *Policing and Society*, vol. 11, 2001, p. 152.

II. Oversight of lawyers and prosecutors

Given the crucial role that they play in criminal justice systems and, in particular, in shaping the response of those systems to terrorism, lawyers and prosecutors must be kept accountable by maintaining the highest standards of probity and professional integrity. Independent and effective mechanisms must also be in place to monitor the application of those standards.

Principle 14 of the Basic Principles on the Role of Lawyers makes it clear that "lawyers in protecting the rights of their clients and in promoting the cause of justice, shall seek to uphold human rights and fundamental freedoms recognized by national and international law and shall at all times act freely and diligently in accordance with the law and recognized standards and ethics of the legal profession". According to the Basic Principles, lawyers must always loyally respect the interests of their clients.

Codes of professional conduct for lawyers must be established by the legal profession through its appropriate organs, or by means of legislation, in accordance with national law and custom and recognized international standards and norms. Principles 27-29 of the Basic Principles on the Role of Lawyers also provide guidance on the conduct of disciplinary proceedings when charges or complaints are made against lawyers:

> "27. Charges or complaints made against lawyers in their professional capacity shall be processed expeditiously and fairly under appropriate procedures. Lawyers shall have the right to a fair hearing, including the right to be assisted by a lawyer of their choice.

> "28. Disciplinary proceedings against lawyers shall be brought before an impartial disciplinary committee established by the legal profession, before an independent statutory authority, or before a court, and shall be subject to an independent judicial review.

> "29. All disciplinary proceedings shall be determined in accordance with the code of professional conduct and other recognized standards and ethics of the legal profession and in the light of these principles."

Prosecutors must, in accordance with the law, perform their duties fairly, consistently and expeditiously and respect and protect human dignity and uphold human rights.

Guideline No. 13 of the Guidelines on the Role of Prosecutors, makes some of those duties explicit:

> "13. In the performance of their duties, prosecutors shall:

> "*(a)* Carry out their functions impartially and avoid all political, social, religious, racial, cultural, sexual or any other kind of discrimination;

> "*(b)* Protect the public interest, act with objectivity, take proper account of the position of the suspect and the victim, and pay attention to all relevant circumstances, irrespective of whether they are to the advantage or disadvantage of the suspect;

"*(c)* Keep matters in their possession confidential, unless the performance of duty or the needs of justice require otherwise;

"*(d)* Consider the views and concerns of victims when their personal interests are affected and ensure that victims are informed of their rights in accordance with the Declaration of Basic Principles of Justice for Victims of Crime and Abuse of Power."

Guideline No. 21 of the Guidelines on the Role of Prosecutors stipulates that "disciplinary offences of prosecutors shall be based on law or lawful regulations. Complaints against prosecutors which allege that they acted in a manner clearly out of the range of professional standards shall be processed expeditiously and fairly under appropriate procedures. Prosecutors shall have the right to a fair hearing. The decision shall be subject to independent review."

Guideline No. 22 adds that "disciplinary proceedings against prosecutors shall guarantee an objective evaluation and decision. They shall be determined in accordance with the law, the code of professional conduct and other established standards and ethics and in the light of the present Guidelines."

Guideline No. 17 states that "in countries where prosecutors are vested with discretionary functions, the law or published rules or regulations shall provide guidelines to enhance fairness and consistency of approach in taking decisions in the prosecution process, including institution or waiver of prosecution". In many States, prosecutors continue to have some broad discretionary powers, which are balanced by a requirement for greater public accountability. The establishment and publication of prosecutorial priorities, guidelines and codes of ethics are essential steps toward greater transparency and accountability with respect to prosecutors and the decisions that they make.

Given the limited resources at their disposal and the rapidly increasing costs of prosecution, prosecutors must frequently make decisions based partly on cost considerations rather than strictly on legal considerations. The high cost of international cases, the complexity of cases and, in some cases, the evidentiary material involved render a certain amount of discretionary decision-making inevitable in these matters. Rule-of-law considerations must nevertheless guide decision-making, and that can present difficult challenges for prosecution services and their managers. Prosecutorial decisions, particularly where there is room for considerable discretion, create room for corruption and discrimination unless those decisions are subjected to public scrutiny and review by appropriate authorities.

Transparency in prosecutorial decision-making, to the extent possible under national law and consistent with the principles of the rule of law, is necessary to reveal and mitigate the potential shortcomings of prosecutorial decisions. Furthermore, fair, just and credible prosecution practices can be encouraged through the development of prosecutorial policies, the identification and publication of prosecutorial priorities and the encouragement of public input. All aspects of prosecutorial policies, tactics and strategies cannot be placed in the public domain, because publicity may defeat their original purpose. However, the appropriate level of transparency can certainly be an antidote to the misuse of discretionary powers, which can weaken the principle of the rule of law and thus undermine the legitimacy of the legal system. Finally, empirical studies, independent reviews and the publication of findings on the use of prosecutorial discretion can provide a basis for a healthy measure of public scrutiny and discussion.

The continuous training of prosecutors also contributes to the creation of a workgroup culture in which the risks of abusive, inconsistent or unfair prosecutorial actions are understood. In other words, prosecutors ought not lose sight of the damage to their own future work caused by improper actions even against defendants for serious crimes. Such risks are quite apparent in recent counter-terrorism policies and practices.

III. Oversight of the judiciary

A process must be established by law to deal with complaints and allegations of misconduct by members of the judiciary, without compromising the independence of the judiciary. Principles 17-20 of the Basic Principles on the Independence of the Judiciary provide guidance for the fair and appropriate investigation of judges and responses to complaints or allegations made against judges:

> "17. A charge or complaint made against a judge in his/her judicial and professional capacity shall be processed expeditiously and fairly under an appropriate procedure. The judge shall have the right to a fair hearing. The examination of the matter at its initial stage shall be kept confidential, unless otherwise requested by the judge.

> "18. Judges shall be subject to suspension or removal only for reasons of incapacity or behaviour that renders them unfit to discharge their duties.

> "19. All disciplinary, suspension or removal proceedings shall be determined in accordance with established standards of judicial conduct.

> "20. Decisions in disciplinary, suspension or removal proceedings should be subject to an independent review. This principle may not apply to the decisions of the highest court and those of the legislature in impeachment or similar proceedings."

As noted above, the Bangalore Principles of Judicial Conduct[171] establish the standards for the ethical conduct of judges and provide guidance to judges, as well as a framework for the regulation of judicial conduct and the response to incidents of judicial misconduct.

---

[171]E/CN.4/2003/65, annex.

IV. Prison oversight and inspections

The nature of inspections carried out in prisons varies from country to country. However, most correctional systems provide for both an internal and an external inspection process. National external inspection bodies may include commissions or persons appointed by the Government, human rights commissions, inspection bodies appointed by the Parliament, ombudsmen and lay inspection bodies (sometimes referred to as monitoring boards). In some countries, there is a special judge with responsibility for prison inspections. In other countries, there are supervision boards at the local level, often headed by a judge.

Standard Minimum Rules for the Treatment of Prisoners

55. There shall be a regular inspection of penal institutions and services by qualified and experienced inspectors appointed by a competent authority. Their task shall be in particular to ensure that these institutions are administered in accordance with existing laws and regulations and with a view to bringing about the objectives of penal and correctional services.

Inspectors appointed by the ministry responsible may carry out internal inspections, as may bodies responsible for administrative inspections. Prison inspections may also be carried out by external bodies responsible for inspections in a variety of activities outside prisons. Such inspections may relate to sanitation, preparation of food, medical services, health and safety in prison industries and fire prevention, among other things. Such inspection bodies may belong to ministries other than the ministry responsible for prisons, which helps ensure the independence and objectivity of the inspection and reporting.

Inspections may also be carried out by international and regional bodies such as the Special Rapporteur of the Human Rights Council on torture and other cruel, inhuman or degrading treatment or punishment, the European Committee for the Prevention of Torture and Inhuman or Degrading Treatment or Punishment of the Council of Europe and the International Committee of the Red Cross.

Independent inspection and monitoring is a basic and essential element of ensuring compliance with human rights in prison systems. The practice of external independent inspections highlights abuses, protects prison staff from unfounded criticism, strengthens the hand of staff who want to resist involvement in brutality and, if such reports are published, helps to keep the challenges of prison reform in the public eye.

Conclusion

The United Nations Global Counter-Terrorism Strategy underscores the international community's recognition that an effective and durable counter-terrorism strategy must focus on several key areas, including addressing the conditions conducive to the spread of terrorism, the development of the capacity of States to prevent and combat terrorism, and unwavering respect for human rights, due process and the rule of law. The Strategy neatly brings those essential elements together in a single document, with global support. Strengthening the capacity of the criminal justice systems of Member States to appropriately investigate, prosecute and adjudicate terrorist cases is an important component of this comprehensive strategy.

Strong criminal justice systems, underpinned by appropriate laws and specialized capacity, are essential to enabling States to comply with their legal obligations under the universal regime against terrorism, including the legal instruments to which they are party and the legally binding obligations stemming from the relevant Security Council resolutions. Indeed, the improved capacity of national criminal justice systems to deal with complex crimes such as terrorism will have positive implications for the system as a whole. The capacity of criminal justice systems to fight terrorism is nearly undistinguishable from its general capacity to respond to other serious crimes within the framework of the rule of law and international human rights law. Even in a situation of relative emergency created by a specific terrorist threat, it is not possible to build the capacity of a justice system to fight terrorist activities without addressing its overall capacity to function as a fair, efficient and accountable system.

The present *Handbook on Criminal Justice Responses to Terrorism* provides some basic guidance to policymakers and practitioners on how to go about building the capacity of their justice system to prevent and counter terrorism. It does not cover every aspect of the task in detail and it does not provide easy, one-size-fits-all recipes. However, when used in combination with other assistance tools, it should provide a useful starting point. A list of other useful tools is contained in the annex.